advantage interactive cd-rom

_____

_____

_____

Place
Postage
Here

Irwin/McGraw-Hill
Attn: Jim Rogers, Marketing Manager
1333 Burr Ridge Parkway
Burr Ridge, IL 60521

Microsoft® PowerPoint® 97 for Windows®

Sarah E. Hutchinson

Glen J. Coulthard

THE IRWIN/MCGRAW-HILL ADVANTAGE SERIES FOR COMPUTER EDUCATION

Irwin
McGraw-Hill

Boston, Massachusetts Burr Ridge, Illinois Dubuque, Iowa
Madison, Wisconsin New York, New York San Francisco, California St. Louis, Missouri

Irwin/McGraw-Hill

A Division of The **McGraw·Hill** Companies

MICROSOFT® POWERPOINT® 97 for WINDOWS®

Copyright © 1997 by The McGraw-Hill Companies, Inc. All rights reserved. Printed in the United States of America. Except as permitted under the United States Copyright Act of 1976, no part of this publication may be reproduced or distributed in any form or by any means, or stored in a data base or retrieval system, without the prior written permission of the publisher.

This book is printed on acid-free paper.

2 3 4 5 6 7 8 9 0 WC/WC 9 0 9 8 7

ISBN 0-256-26001-X

Publisher: *Tom Casson*
Sponsoring editor: *Garrett Glanz*
Developmental editor: *Kristin Hepburn*
GTS production coordinator: *Cathy Stotts*
Marketing manager: *James Rogers*
Senior project supervisor: *Denise Santor-Mitzit*
Production supervisor: *Pat Frederickson*
Art director: *Keith McPherson*
Prepress buyer: *Heather D. Burbridge*
Compositor: *GTS Graphics, Inc.*
Typeface: *11/13 Bodoni Book*
Printer: *Webcrafters, Inc.*

http://www.mhcollege.com

WELCOME TO THE IRWIN ADVANTAGE SERIES

The Irwin Advantage Series has evolved over the years to become one of the most respected resources for software training in the world—to date, over 200,000 students have used one or more of our learning guides. Our instructional methodologies are proven to optimize the student's ability to learn, yet we continually seek ways to improve on our products and approach. To this end, all of our learning guides are classroom tested and critically reviewed by dozens of learners, teachers, and software training experts. We're glad you have chosen the Irwin Advantage Series!

KEY FEATURES

The following features are incorporated into the new Microsoft Office 97 student learning guides to ensure that your learning experience is as productive and enjoyable as possible:

CASE STUDIES

Each session begins with a real-world **case study** that introduces you to a fictitious person or company and describes their immediate problem or opportunity. Throughout the session, you obtain the knowledge and skills necessary to meet these challenges. At the end of the session, you are given an opportunity to solve **case problems** directly related to the case scenario.

CONCEPTS, SKILLS AND PROCEDURES

Each learning guide organizes and presents its content in logically structured session topics. Commands and procedures are introduced using **hands-on examples in a step-by-step format,** and students are encouraged to perform the steps along with the guide. These examples are clearly identified by the text design.

PERFORM THE FOLLOWING STEPS

Using this new design feature, the step progression for all hands-on examples and exercises are clearly identified. Students will find it surprisingly easy to follow the logical sequence of keystrokes and mouse clicks. No longer do you have to worry about missing a step!

END OF SESSION EXERCISES

Each session concludes with **short answer questions** and **hands-on exercises.** These comprehensive and meaningful exercises are integrated with the session's objectives; they were not added as an afterthought. They serve to provide students with opportunities to practice the session material. For maximum benefit, students should complete all the exercises at the end of each session.

IN ADDITION BOXES

These content boxes are placed strategically throughout the guide and provide information on related topics that are beyond the scope of the current discussion. For example, there are three typical categories that are visually identified by the following icons:

Integration
The key to productive and efficient use of Office 97 is in the integration features for sharing data among the applications. With a few mouse clicks, for example, you can create a PowerPoint presentation from a Word document, copy an Access database into an Excel workbook, and incorporate professional Office Art into your annual report. Under this heading, you will find methods for sharing information among the Microsoft Office 97 applications.

Advanced
In a 200+-page learning guide, there are bound to be features that are important but beyond the scope of the text. Therefore, we call attention to these features and offer suggestions on how to apply techniques or to search for more information.

Internet
The Internet is fast becoming a standard tool for gathering and exchanging information. Office 97 provides a high level of Internet connectivity, allowing the user to draw upon its vast resources and even publish documents directly on the World Wide Web. Although not every student will have a persistent Internet connection, you can review the content under this heading to learn about Office's Internet features.

Real life situations
introduce the topics →

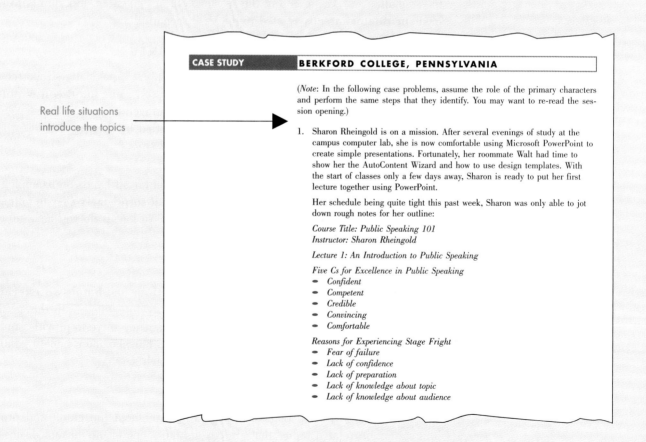

| CASE STUDY | BERKFORD COLLEGE, PENNSYLVANIA |

(*Note*: In the following case problems, assume the role of the primary characters and perform the same steps that they identify. You may want to re-read the session opening.)

1. Sharon Rheingold is on a mission. After several evenings of study at the campus computer lab, she is now comfortable using Microsoft PowerPoint to create simple presentations. Fortunately, her roommate Walt had time to show her the AutoContent Wizard and how to use design templates. With the start of classes only a few days away, Sharon is ready to put her first lecture together using PowerPoint.

    Her schedule being quite tight this past week, Sharon was only able to jot down rough notes for her outline:

    Course Title: Public Speaking 101
    Instructor: Sharon Rheingold

    Lecture 1: An Introduction to Public Speaking

    Five Cs for Excellence in Public Speaking
    - *Confident*
    - *Competent*
    - *Credible*
    - *Convincing*
    - *Comfortable*

    Reasons for Experiencing Stage Fright
    - *Fear of failure*
    - *Lack of confidence*
    - *Lack of preparation*
    - *Lack of knowledge about topic*
    - *Lack of knowledge about audience*

Large figures guide
learning

Easy to read and
identify step-by-step
instructions

In Addition boxes
expand on topics

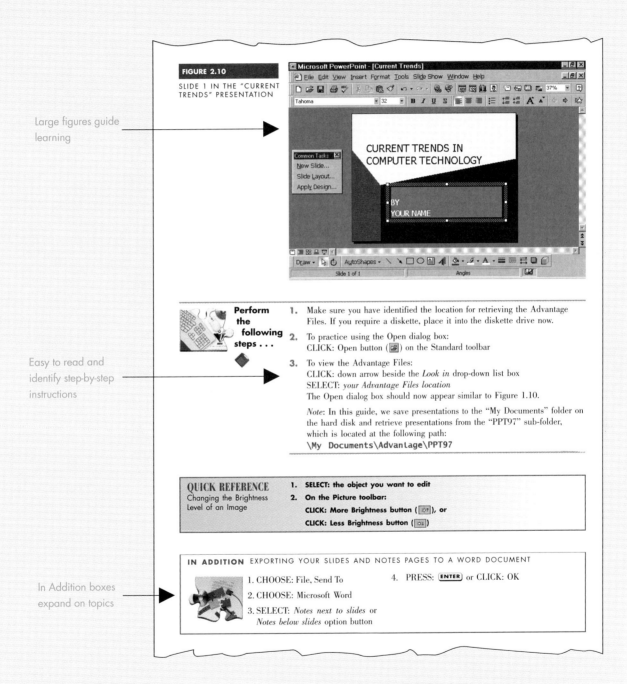

FIGURE 2.10

SLIDE 1 IN THE "CURRENT
TRENDS" PRESENTATION

**Perform
the
following
steps . . .**

1. Make sure you have identified the location for retrieving the Advantage Files. If you require a diskette, place it into the diskette drive now.

2. To practice using the Open dialog box:
CLICK: Open button (📂) on the Standard toolbar

3. To view the Advantage Files:
CLICK: down arrow beside the *Look in* drop-down list box
SELECT: *your Advantage Files location*
The Open dialog box should now appear similar to Figure 1.10.

Note: In this guide, we save presentations to the "My Documents" folder on the hard disk and retrieve presentations from the "PPT97" sub-folder, which is located at the following path:
`\My Documents\Advantage\PPT97`

QUICK REFERENCE
Changing the Brightness
Level of an Image

1. **SELECT: the object you want to edit**
2. **On the Picture toolbar:**
CLICK: More Brightness button (☼), or
CLICK: Less Brightness button (☼)

IN ADDITION EXPORTING YOUR SLIDES AND NOTES PAGES TO A WORD DOCUMENT

1. CHOOSE: File, Send To
2. CHOOSE: Microsoft Word
3. SELECT: *Notes next to slides* or *Notes below slides* option button

4. PRESS: [ENTER] or CLICK: OK

Students practice with
real life projects

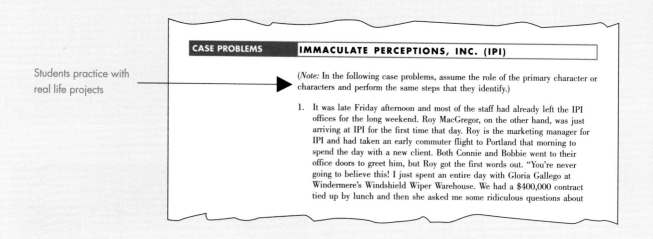

CASE PROBLEMS   IMMACULATE PERCEPTIONS, INC. (IPI)

(*Note:* In the following case problems, assume the role of the primary character or characters and perform the same steps that they identify.)

1. It was late Friday afternoon and most of the staff had already left the IPI offices for the long weekend. Roy MacGregor, on the other hand, was just arriving at IPI for the first time that day. Roy is the marketing manager for IPI and had taken an early commuter flight to Portland that morning to spend the day with a new client. Both Connie and Bobbie went to their office doors to greet him, but Roy got the first words out. "You're never going to believe this! I just spent an entire day with Gloria Gallego at Windermere's Windshield Wiper Warehouse. We had a $400,000 contract tied up by lunch and then she asked me some ridiculous questions about

TEXT SUPPLEMENTS

ADVANTAGE FILES

Certain hands-on examples and exercises are marked with a disk ◆ icon, indicating the need to retrieve a document file from the **Advantage Files location.** These document files may be provided to you in a number of ways: packaged on a diskette accompanying this text, or on the computer network at your school. You may also download the files from the **Advantage Online** Web site (http://www.irwin.com/cit/adv). *These documents files are extremely important to your success.* Check with your instructor or lab advisor for details on how to acquire the Advantage Files.

In addition to identifying the Advantage Files location, you will also need to specify a **Data Files location.** This location is used to save the documents that you create and may either be a blank diskette or a folder on the network server. Again, your instructor or lab advisor will specify the proper locations. More information on the file locations and the proper techniques for retrieving and saving information is provided inside the back cover of this book.

CD-ROM INTERACTIVE TUTORIALS

In addition to using this book, you may have access to our *Advantage Interactive* software. These interactive multimedia tutorials are fully integrated with the material from each session and make effective use of video clips, screen demonstrations, hands-on exercises, and quizzes. You will enjoy the opportunity to explore these tutorials and learn the software at your own pace. For ordering information, please refer to the coupon inside the front cover.

INSTRUCTOR'S RESOURCE KIT

For instructors and software trainers, each learning guide is accompanied by an **Instructor's Resource Kit (IRK).** This kit provides suggested answers to the short-answer questions, hands-on exercises, and case problems appearing at the end of each session. Furthermore, the IRK includes a comprehensive test bank of additional short-answer, multiple-choice, and fill-in-the-blank questions, plus hands-on exercises. You will also find a diskette copy of the Advantage Files which may be duplicated or placed on your network for student use.

SUPPORT THROUGH THE WWW

The Internet, and more specifically the World Wide Web, is an important component in our approach to software instruction for the Office 97 application series. The *Advantage Online* site at http://www.irwin.com/cit/adv is a tremendous resource for all users, providing information on the latest software and learning guide releases, download options for the Advantage Files, and supplemental files for the Instructor Resource Kits. We also introduce new methods for you to communicate with the authors, publisher, and other users of the series. As a dynamic venture, *Advantage Online* will evolve and improve over time. Please visit us to see the latest developments and contribute your valuable feedback.

NETWORK TESTING

Evaluation and assessment are important components of any instructional series. We are committed to providing quality alternatives to traditional testing instruments. With our Irwin Network Test Interactive software, instructors can select questions, create and administer tests, and then calculate grades—all on-line! Visit the *Advantage Online* site for more information on how we are progressing in this exciting area.

Before you begin

As with any software instruction guide, there are standard conventions that we use to indicate menu options, keystroke combinations, and command instructions.

MENU INSTRUCTIONS

In Office 97, all Menu bar options and pull-down menu commands have an underlined or highlighted letter in each option. When you need to execute a command from the Menu bar—the row of menu choices across the top of the screen—the tutorial's instruction line separates the Menu bar option from the command with a comma. Notice also that the word "CHOOSE" is always used for menu commands. For example, the command for quitting Windows is shown as:

CHOOSE: File, Exit

This instruction tells you to choose the File option on the Menu bar and then to choose the Exit command from the File pull-down menu. The actual steps for choosing a menu command are discussed later in this guide.

KEYSTROKES AND KEYSTROKE COMBINATIONS

When two keys must be pressed together, the tutorial's instruction line shows the keys joined with a plus (+) sign. For example, you can execute a Copy command in Windows by holding down [CTRL] and then pressing the letter c.

The instruction for this type of keystroke combination follows:

PRESS: [CTRL]+c

COMMAND INSTRUCTIONS

This guide indicates with a special typeface and color the data that you are required to type in yourself. For example:

TYPE: Income Statement

When you are required to enter unique information, such as the current date or your name, the instruction appears in italic. The following instruction directs you to type your name in place of the actual words: "your name."

TYPE: *your name*

ACKNOWLEDGMENTS

This series of learning guides is the direct result of the teamwork and heart of many people. We sincerely thank the reviewers, instructors, and students who have shared their comments and suggestions with us over the past few years. We do read them! With this valuable feedback, our guides have evolved into the product you see before you. We also appreciate the efforts of the instructors and students at Okanagan University College who classroom tested our guides to ensure accuracy, relevancy, and completeness.

We also give many thanks to Garrett Glanz, Kristin Hepburn and Tom Casson from Irwin for their skillful management of this text. In fact, special recognition goes to all of the individuals mentioned in the credits at the beginning of this guide. And finally, to the many others who weren't directly involved in this project but who have stood by us the whole way, we appreciate your encouragement and support.

WRITE TO US

We welcome your response to this book, for we are trying to make it as useful a learning tool as possible. Write to us in care of Garrett Glanz, Richard D. Irwin, 1333 Burr Ridge Parkway, Burr Ridge, IL 60521. Thank you.

Sarah E. Hutchinson
sclifford@mindspring.com

Glen J. Coulthard
current@junction.net

Contents

SESSION 1
Fundamentals 97

SESSION 2
Creating a Presentation

SESSION 3
Designing a Presentation

SESSION 4
Adding Visual Effects

SESSION 5
Notes, Handouts, and Printing

APPENDIX
Toolbar Summary 169

INDEX   173

Microsoft PowerPoint 97 for Windows

Fundamentals

SESSION OUTLINE

INTRODUCTION

Welcome to Microsoft PowerPoint 97 for Windows, a software program that helps you organize and present information to an audience. You can use PowerPoint to create overhead transparencies, 35 mm slides, audience handouts and speaker's notes, and computer-based slide presentations. PowerPoint also provides tools that help you outline your thoughts, build a presentation quickly using professionally designed templates, and enhance your presentation with pictures, charts, sound, and video.

CASE STUDY	VACATION VISTAS, INC.

Owned by Frank Muldanno, Vacation Vistas of Memphis is a tour operation specializing in Caribbean cruises. For the past eight months, business has been extremely slow. To increase demand for their cruises, Frank believes that he and his staff must direct more of their marketing to the local seniors community.

One of Frank's new marketing tactics was to hire Juanita Gomez, a local computer consultant and graphic designer, to produce a 35 mm slide presentation that he could show at the neighborhood seniors' hall. Halfway through developing the presentation, Juanita accepted a job in Seattle but promised to send Frank the completed slides from the West Coast.

One week before the presentation, Frank receives a disk and a letter from Juanita with the following note: *"Dear Frank, please review the enclosed presentation and send the disk back to me for final production of the 35 mm slides. By the way, the presentation was created using Microsoft PowerPoint. Good luck, Juanita."* Fortunately, Frank has recently purchased Microsoft Office, which includes PowerPoint, for his new office computer. Although he hasn't used the program before, he is relatively comfortable using Windows.

In this session, you and Frank will learn how to load and exit Microsoft Power-Point and how to open and close an existing presentation. You'll also take a guided tour of the screen and learn how to access the Help facility. Lastly, you will experiment with the different methods of viewing a presentation in PowerPoint.

INTRODUCING MICROSOFT OFFICE 97

Microsoft Office for Windows combines the most popular and exciting software programs available into a single suite of applications. In the Professional edition, Office 97 includes Microsoft Word, Microsoft Excel, Microsoft PowerPoint, Microsoft Access, and the all-new Microsoft Outlook, an integrated desktop information tool that manages your e-mail, calendar, contacts, to do lists, journal, and Office documents. Office 97 also provides shared applications (sometimes called "server applications") that let you create and insert clip art, organizational charts, and mathematical equations into your word processing documents, electronic spreadsheets, and presentations.

In addition to enjoying performance improvements over its predecessor, Office 97 offers integration with the Internet and World Wide Web (WWW) and benefits from many usability enhancements. For example, Office 97 lets you do the following:

- name your documents using up to 250 characters,

- place shortcuts to files directly on the Windows desktop,

- use the Windows Briefcase program to compare and synchronize files,

- multitask applications with single-click functionality from the taskbar,

- save documents in the web's Hypertext Markup Language (HTML) format, and

- post documents to your internal intranet or to the web.

All of Office's primary applications use Intellisense technology, helping users to focus on their work and not on their software. Examples of Intellisense are automatic spell and grammar checking and wizards that lead you through performing basic and complex tasks. Office 97 offers additional Help features, including an animated character called the Office Assistant who provides helpful tips and suggestions as you work.

INTEGRATION FEATURES

Many would say that the essence of Office 97 is its ability to share data among the suite of applications. For example, you can place an Excel chart in a report that you write using Word, a Word document in a PowerPoint presentation, an Access database in an Excel worksheet, and so on. You can also create and insert objects using shared applications—such as Microsoft Office Art and Microsoft Organization Chart—without ever leaving the current application. Using Microsoft Binder, you can assemble Word, Excel, and PowerPoint documents into a single file for distribution. Binder also allows you to print a collection of documents with consistent headers and footers and with consecutive page numbering.

INTERNET FEATURES

One of the most exciting innovations in Office 97 is its ability to take advantage of the World Wide Web and the Internet. For those of you new to the online world, the **Internet** is a vast collection of computer networks that spans the entire planet, made up of many smaller networks connected by standard telephone lines. The term **Intranet** is used to refer to a local or wide area network that uses Internet technologies to share information within an organization. To access the Internet, you need a network or modem connection that links your computer to an account on the university's network or to an independent Internet Service Provider (ISP).

Once connected, you use web browser software, such as Microsoft Internet Explorer or Netscape Navigator, to access the **World Wide Web (WWW).** The WWW provides a visual interface for the Internet and lets you search for information by simply clicking on highlighted words and images, know as **hyperlinks.** When you click a link, you are telling your web browser to retrieve and then display a page from a web site. Each web page has a unique location or address specified by its *Uniform Resource Locator* or URL. One example of a URL is: http://www.microsoft.com. For more information on the Internet and World Wide Web, visit your local bookstore, campus computing center, or computer users group.

Microsoft Office 97 provides a consistent set of tools for publishing documents, spreadsheets, presentations, and databases to the web and for accessing help directly from Microsoft's web site. Specifically, each Office application includes a

Web toolbar that lets you quickly open, search, and browse documents on your local computer, Intranet, and the Internet. Furthermore, you can create your own hyperlinks and share your documents with the entire world after publishing it to a web server. As you proceed through this manual, look for the Internet features found in the *In Addition* boxes.

CREATING PRESENTATIONS WITH POWERPOINT

Microsoft PowerPoint is a software program that enables you to produce high-quality output, such as overhead transparencies, 35 mm slides, and computer-based displays, for presentation to an audience. Even if you don't consider yourself a speechwriter or graphics designer, you can still create informative and attractive presentations using PowerPoint. In PowerPoint, a **presentation** is the collection of slides, handouts, speaker's notes, and outlines contained in a single disk file. Below we describe these presentation elements and some additional PowerPoint features:

- *Slides.* A PowerPoint **slide** is an individual page in your presentation. Figure 1.1 shows a sample slide. You can output the slides on your printer as overhead transparencies or send your presentation file on a diskette to an outside service bureau to develop 35 mm slides. A more fashionable option is to display your PowerPoint presentation on a computer monitor or use a projection unit (or LCD panel) and a large projection screen.

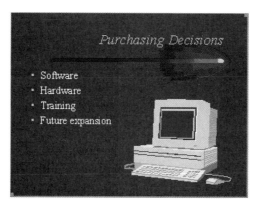

- *Handouts.* A **handout** consists of two to six slide images printed on a single page. Handouts help support your presentation by keeping the audience focused on what you are saying and by not requiring them to write down everything they see on the projection screen.

- *Speaker's notes.* To assist you in the actual delivery of a presentation, PowerPoint lets you enter and print a notes page for each slide.

- *Outlines.* For brainstorming and organizing your thoughts, PowerPoint's outline feature is extremely valuable. In outline form, the text of your presentation—that is, headings and main body text—appears without the slide's background, colors, or graphics.

- *Templates.* For those people who may question their creative and artistic talent, there is absolutely nothing to worry about—PowerPoint provides over 100 professionally designed templates containing proven layouts, color schemes, background textures, and typefaces. A **template** defines what your presentation will look like, where text and other objects will appear, and which foreground and background colors will be used.

- *"Auto" features.* Several "Auto" features make it easier for you to perform your work. For example, PowerPoint's AutoCorrect feature will automatically replace "teh" with "the" and "ast he" with "as the" and ensure that your sentences begin with an uppercase letter. Also, when automatic spell checking is enabled, misspelled words are marked with a red wavy underline. To correct the spelling mistake, you right-click the wavy underline and then choose an option from the shortcut menu. The AutoClipArt command provides suggestions on which pictures to include in your presentation to better convey your message.

- *Wizards.* As you will see in this learning guide, PowerPoint employs many **wizards** to help you get your work done. These software features make short order of the tasks that might otherwise be repetitive, time-consuming, or difficult.

- *The Office Assistant.* Think of the Office Assistant, a component of PowerPoint's Help system, as your own personal computer guru. When you have a question about how to accomplish a task in PowerPoint, you can "talk" to the Office Assistant using typed English phrases. The Office Assistant analyzes your request and provides a resource list of potential help topics. The Assistant can also provide step-by-step instructions on how to complete a task and can even perform certain tasks for you.

- *PowerPoint Central.* PowerPoint Central is an online magazine, or electronic slide show, that is automatically installed on your computer as part of a typical PowerPoint 97 installation. In it, you can find suggestions and tips for using PowerPoint and creating effective presentations. Also, it provides an additional resource for templates, sounds, animation clips, and other types of objects that you might want to include in a presentation.

- *PowerPoint Viewer.* Microsoft PowerPoint includes a **run-time version** of the program called the PowerPoint Viewer. You can create a presentation on your computer and then send it along on a diskette with the PowerPoint Viewer to your employees, clients, students, or other recipients who do not own Microsoft PowerPoint. As long as they have Microsoft Windows installed on their computers, the recipients of your diskettes will be able to view (but not change) your presentation using the Viewer.

Now, let's begin our journey through Microsoft PowerPoint 97.

STARTING POWERPOINT

This session assumes that you are working on a computer with Windows and Microsoft PowerPoint 97 loaded on the hard disk drive. Before you load Windows and PowerPoint, let's look at how to use the mouse and keyboard.

USING THE MOUSE AND KEYBOARD

Microsoft PowerPoint 97 for Windows is a complex yet easy-to-learn program. As you proceed through this guide, you will find that there are often three methods for performing the same command or procedure in Word:

- Menu   Select a command or procedure from the Menu bar.

- Mouse   Point to and click a toolbar button or use the Ruler.

- Keyboard   Press a keyboard shortcut (usually (CTRL)+letter).

Although this guide concentrates on the quickest and easiest methods, we recommend that you try the others and decide which you prefer. *Don't memorize all of the methods and information in this guide! Be selective and find your favorite methods.*

Although you may use PowerPoint with only a keyboard, much of the program's basic design relies on using a mouse. Regardless of whether your mouse has two or three buttons, you use the left or primary mouse button for selecting text and menu commands and the right or secondary mouse button for displaying shortcut menus. The most common mouse actions used in PowerPoint are listed below:

- Point   Slide the mouse on your desk to position the tip of the mouse pointer over the desired object on the screen.

- Click   Press down and release the left mouse button quickly. Clicking is used to position the insertion point, choose menu commands, and make selections in a dialog box.

- Right-Click   Press down and release the right mouse button. Right-clicking the mouse on text or an object displays a context-sensitive shortcut menu.

- Double-Click   Press down and release the mouse button twice in rapid succession. Double-clicking is often used in PowerPoint to select and execute an action.

- Drag   Press down and hold the mouse button as you move the mouse pointer across the screen. When the mouse pointer reaches the desired location, release the mouse button. Dragging is used to select a block of text or to move objects or windows.

You may notice that the mouse pointer changes shape as you move it over different parts of the screen or during processing. Each mouse pointer shape has its own purpose and may provide you with important information. There are five primary mouse shapes you should be aware of:

↖	left arrow	Used to choose menu commands, access the toolbars, and make selections in dialog boxes.
⧗	Hourglass	Informs you that PowerPoint is occupied with another task and requests that you wait.
I	I-beam	Used to modify and edit text and to position the insertion point.
☝	Hand	In a Help window, the hand is used to select shortcuts and definitions.

As you proceed through this guide, other mouse shapes will be explained in the appropriate sections.

Aside from being the primary input device for entering text in a presentation, the keyboard offers shortcut methods for performing commands and procedures. For example, several menu commands have shortcut key combinations listed to the right of the command in the pull-down menu. Therefore, you can perform a command by simply pressing the shortcut keys rather than accessing the Menu bar. Many of these shortcut key combinations are available throughout Windows applications.

LOADING WINDOWS

Because Windows is an operating system, it is loaded automatically into the computer's memory when you turn on the computer. In this section, you turn your computer on to load Windows.

Perform the following steps . . .

1. Turn on the power switches to the computer and monitor. After a few seconds, the Windows desktop will appear (Figure 1.2). (*Note:* The desktop interface on your computer may look different from Figure 1.2.)

2. If a Welcome to Windows dialog box appears, do the following:
   CLICK: Close button ([✖]) in the top right-hand corner of the window

FIGURE 1.2

THE WINDOWS DESKTOP

QUICK REFERENCE	Turn on your computer to load Microsoft Windows (or Microsoft Windows NT
Loading Windows	**3.51 or later).**

LOADING MICROSOFT POWERPOINT 97

In this section, you load Microsoft PowerPoint.

Perform the following steps . . .

1. Point to the Start button (**Start**) on the taskbar and then click the left mouse button once. The Start menu appears as a pop-up menu.

2. Point to the Programs command using the mouse. Notice that you do not need to click the left mouse button to display the list of programs in the fly-out or cascading menu.

3. Move the mouse pointer horizontally to the right until it highlights an option in the Programs menu. You can now move the mouse pointer up and down the Programs menu. Notice that you still haven't clicked the left mouse button.

4. Point to the Microsoft PowerPoint menu item and then click the left mouse button once to execute the command. After a few seconds, the Microsoft PowerPoint screen appears.

5. If the Office Assistant (shown at the right) appears:
   CLICK: Close button (☒) in its top right-hand corner

6. The PowerPoint startup dialog box should appear on your screen (Figure 1.3). You use this dialog box to determine how you want to proceed when PowerPoint is first loaded. (*Note:* You can turn this feature off using the Tools, Options command. For this guide, we leave the startup dialog box displayed.) As shown in Figure 1.3, the Common Tasks toolbar may also appear on your screen. We describe the Common Tasks toolbar shortly.

FIGURE 1.3

THE POWERPOINT
STARTUP DIALOG BOX
AND THE COMMON
TASKS TOOLBAR

7. Before continuing, let's temporarily remove the startup dialog box so that we can describe the components of PowerPoint in the next section. We will return to the options available in the startup dialog box later. Do the following:
   CLICK: Cancel command button
   (*Note:* The word CLICK means to point to the command button and then click the left mouse button once.) The Common Tasks toolbar may still appear on your screen.

QUICK REFERENCE Loading Microsoft PowerPoint 97	1. CLICK: Start button (Start) 2. CHOOSE: Programs, Microsoft PowerPoint

THE GUIDED TOUR

Software programs designed for Microsoft Windows, such as PowerPoint, have many similarities in screen design and layout. Each program operates in its own application window, while the presentations, spreadsheets, and letters you create appear in separate document windows. In PowerPoint, the document window is referred to as the presentation window. This section explores the various parts of PowerPoint, including the tools for manipulating application and presentation windows.

APPLICATION WINDOW

The PowerPoint screen consists of the **application window** and the **presentation window.** The application window (Figure 1.4) contains the Title bar, Menu bar, Standard toolbar, Formatting toolbar, Drawing toolbar, Status bar, and Slide work area. Presentation windows contain the actual slide presentations that you create and store on the disk.

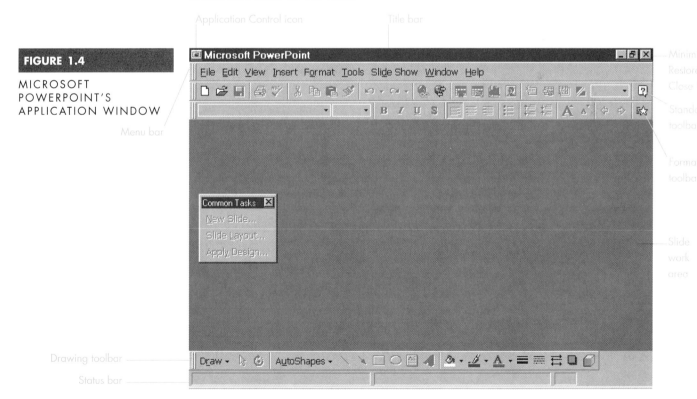

FIGURE 1.4

MICROSOFT POWERPOINT'S APPLICATION WINDOW

The primary components of the application window are listed below:

Application Control icon (▣)	Used to size and position the application window using the keyboard. (*Note:* It is easier to use the mouse to perform the same options available in the Control menu.)
Minimize (▬) and Maximize (▢), Restore (▤), and Close (☒) icons	Located in the top right-hand corner of the application window, these icons are used to control the display of the application window using the mouse. (*Note:* The Maximize button doesn't appear in Figure 1.4.)
Title bar	The Title bar contains the name of the program or presentation file. Using a mouse, you can move a window by dragging its Title bar.
Menu bar	Contains the PowerPoint menu commands.
Standard toolbar	The Standard toolbar displays buttons for opening and saving presentations, editing text, and accessing special features using the mouse.
Formatting toolbar	The Formatting toolbar displays buttons for accessing character and paragraph formatting commands using a mouse.
Drawing toolbar	The Drawing toolbar displays buttons for drawing objects such as lines, circles, and boxes.
Status bar	Located at the bottom of the application window and above the taskbar, the Status bar displays the current slide number and a description of the current design template. The Status bar contains information once a presentation is opened.
Slide work area	The Slide work area is where your presentation windows appear. You can work on more than one presentation at the same time in this work area.

Although typically maximized, you can size, move, and manipulate the PowerPoint application window on the Windows desktop to customize your work environment.

PRESENTATION WINDOW

The presentation window provides the viewing and editing area for a presentation. Figure 1.5 shows an example of a presentation window that is not maximized, as it would appear in the Slide work area of PowerPoint's application window. You will open and display a presentation window shortly.

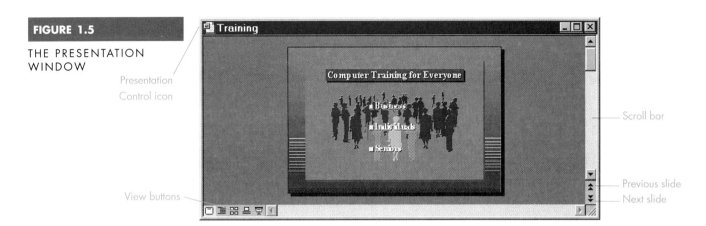

FIGURE 1.5

THE PRESENTATION
WINDOW

Presentation
Control icon

Scroll bar

Previous slide
Next slide

View buttons

The primary components of the presentation window are listed below:

Presentation Control icon (⊞)	Used to size and position the application window using the keyboard. (*Note:* It is easier to use a mouse to perform the same options available in the Presentation Control menu.)
Scroll bar	Placed at the right border of the presentation window, the vertical scroll bar facilitates moving from slide to slide using the mouse. As you drag the scroll box or elevator up and down, the current slide number displays in a Slide number box along the scroll bar.
Previous slide (⏫), Next slide (⏬)	Use these buttons to display the previous slide or the next slide.
View buttons	Located at the bottom left-hand corner of the presentation window, the View buttons let you change the current view of the presentation.

You should recognize some familiar components in the presentation window that appear in all windows. For example, the Minimize and Maximize icons appear in the top right-hand corner of the presentation window. To restore a maximized presentation to a window, you click the Restore icon (🗗). To maximize the presentation window, you click the Maximize icon (🗖). Before proceeding, make sure that your application and presentation windows are maximized.

MENU BAR

PowerPoint commands are grouped together on the Menu bar, as shown below.

File Edit View Insert Format Tools Slide Show Window Help

Commands in this guide are written in the following form: Edit, Copy, where Edit is the Menu bar option and Copy is the command to be selected from the pull-down menu. To execute a command, click once on the Menu bar option and then click once on the pull-down menu command. Commands that are not available for selection appear dimmed. Commands that are followed by an ellipsis (...) require further information to be collected in a dialog box. If you choose a command that is followed by a sideways triangle (▶), an additional pull-down menu will appear.

Now you will practice accessing the Menu bar.

Perform the following steps . . .

1. To choose the Help command, position the tip of the mouse pointer on the word Help in the Menu bar and click the left mouse button once. A pull-down menu appears below the Help option.

2. To see the pull-down menu associated with the File menu option, point to the File option on the Menu bar.

3. To leave the Menu bar without making a selection:
   CLICK: anywhere in the Slide work area
   (*Note:* Also, clicking the menu option again, clicking the Title bar, or pressing ⌐ESC⌐ removes the pull-down menu.)

4. To again display the pull-down menu for the File option:
   CHOOSE: File
   This instruction tells you to click the mouse pointer on File in the Menu bar. (*Note:* All menu commands that you execute in this guide begin with the word "CHOOSE.")

5. To again leave the Menu bar without making a selection:
   CHOOSE: File

SHORTCUT MENUS

PowerPoint uses context-sensitive shortcut menus for quick access to menu commands. Rather than searching for commands in the Menu bar, you position the mouse pointer on text or an object, such as a graphic, and click the right mouse button. A pop-up menu appears with the most commonly selected commands for the text or object.

Now you will practice accessing a shortcut menu.

Perform the following steps . . .

1. To display a shortcut or pop-up menu, position the mouse pointer over any button on the Standard toolbar and click the right mouse button. The shortcut menu at the right should appear.

2. To remove the shortcut menu from the screen, move the mouse pointer into the Slide work area and click the left mouse button. The shortcut menu disappears.

TOOLBARS

Assuming that you haven't yet customized your PowerPoint screen, you will see the Standard and Formatting toolbars appear below the Menu bar. You may also see the Common Tasks toolbar appear somewhere in the Slide work area and the Drawing toolbar appear at the bottom of the application window.

PowerPoint provides eleven toolbars and hundreds of buttons and drop-down lists for quick and easy mouse access to its more popular commands and features. Don't worry about memorizing the button names appearing in the following graphics—the majority of these buttons are explained in subsequent sessions and all toolbars and their buttons are summarized in the Appendix. You can also point at any toolbar button and pause until a yellow ToolTip appears with the button name. With the ToolTip displayed, an extended description for the button appears in the Status bar.

Below we identify the buttons on the Standard and Formatting toolbars. (*Note:* On your computer, many of the buttons on these toolbars appear dimmed, currently unavailable for use. Many will become available once you open a presentation.)

The Standard toolbar provides access to file management and slide editing commands.

The Formatting toolbar lets you access formatting commands.

To display additional toolbars, you point to an existing toolbar and click the right mouse button. From the shortcut menu that appears, you can display and hide toolbars by clicking their names in the pop-up menu. If a toolbar is currently being displayed, a check mark appears beside its name. You can also choose the View, Toolbars command to display the Toolbars menu.

In this section, you practice displaying and hiding toolbars.

 **Perform the following steps . . .**

1. Position the mouse pointer over any button on the Standard toolbar.

2. CLICK: right mouse button to display the shortcut menu

3. To display the Animation Effects toolbar:
   CHOOSE: Animation Effects
   The new toolbar appears in the Slide work area.

4. To remove the Animation Effects toolbar:
   RIGHT-CLICK: Animation Effects toolbar
   This instruction tells you to position the mouse pointer over the Animation Effects toolbar and click the right mouse button.

5. You will notice that the Animation Effects command on the shortcut menu has a check mark. To remove the Animation Effects toolbar:
   CHOOSE: Animation Effects
   The Animation Effects toolbar disappears from the application window.

STATUS BAR

The Status bar provides status information for a presentation, including the current slide number and template description. The Status bar shows that "FANS" is the name of the current template.

| Slide 1 of 3 | FANS | |

To correct all of your spelling errors at once, use the book icon on the Status bar. If your presentation is free of spelling errors, a check mark will appear on the book icon. Otherwise, an "✗" will appear. To jump through the spelling errors in a presentation, double-click the book icon.

DIALOG BOX

A dialog box is a common mechanism in Windows applications for collecting information before processing a command or instruction (Figure 1.6). In a dialog box, you indicate the options you want to use and then click the OK button when you're finished. Dialog boxes are also used to display messages or to ask for confirmation of commands.

A dialog box uses several methods for collecting information, as shown in Figure 1.6 and described in Table 1.1.

FIGURE 1.6

A DIALOG BOX

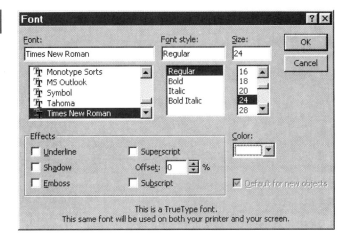

	Name	Example	Action
TABLE 1.1			
Parts of a dialog box	Check box	☑ Always ☐ Never	Click an option to turn it on or off. The option is turned on when an "✓" appears in the box.
	Command button	OK / Cancel	Click a command button to execute an action. You accept or cancel the selections in a dialog box by clicking the OK or Cancel command buttons, respectively.
	Drop-down list box	Screen Saver / None	Make a choice from the list that appears when you click the down arrow next to the box; only the selected choice is visible.
	List box	Wallpaper / (None) / Arcade / Argyle	Make a choice from the scrollable list; several choices, if not all, are always visible.
	Option button	Display: ⦿ Tile ○ Center	Select an option from a group of related options.
	Slide box	Desktop area / Less — More / 640 by 480 pixels	Drag the slider bar to make a selection, like using a radio's volume control.
	Spin box	Wait: 6 minutes	Click the up and down arrows to the right of the box until the number you want appears.

TABLE 1.1	*Name*	*Example*	*Action*
Continued	Tab	General │ Letters & Faxes │	Click a named tab at the top of the window to access other pages of options in the dialog box.
	Text box	File name: untitled	Click inside the text box and then type the desired information.

Most dialog boxes provide a question mark button (**?**) near the right side of the Title bar. If you have a question about an item in the dialog box, click the question mark and then click the item to display some helpful information. You should also know that dialog boxes have a memory. For example, the tab that appears when you exit the dialog box will be selected the next time you open the dialog box.

THE WINDOWS TASKBAR

The Windows taskbar is usually located on the bottom of your screen below the Status bar. (*Note:* We say "usually" because you can move the taskbar on your desktop.) Each application that you are currently working with is represented by a button on the taskbar. To switch between applications, click the appropriate application button on the taskbar. At this point, you should see a button for Microsoft PowerPoint on the taskbar.

GETTING HELP

PowerPoint provides several **context-sensitive help** features and a comprehensive library of online documentation. Like many developers trying to minimize the retail price of software and maximize profits, Microsoft has stopped shipping volumes of print-based documentation in favor of disk-based Help systems. However, a Help system is only as good as the search tools that it provides. Fortunately for us, Windows gives developers the tools and capability to create consistent and easy-to-use Help systems. This section describes the context-sensitive help features found in PowerPoint and then describes where to find more detailed information using the Help Topics window.

CONTEXT-SENSITIVE HELP

Context-sensitive help refers to a software program's ability to retrieve and present helpful information reflecting your current position in the program. In PowerPoint, you can access context-sensitive help for menu options, toolbar buttons, and dialog box items. The help information is presented concisely in a small pop-up window that you can remove with a click of the mouse. This type of help lets you access information quickly and then continue working without interruption. Table 1.2 describes some methods for accessing context-sensitive help while working in PowerPoint.

TABLE 1.2	To display...	Do this...
Displaying context-sensitive Help information	A description of a dialog box item	Click the question mark button (?) in a dialog box's Title bar and then click an item in the dialog box. A helpful description of the item appears in a pop-up window. Additionally, you can often right-click a dialog box item to display its description.
	A description of a menu command	Choose Help, What's This? from the Menu bar and then choose the desired command using the question mark mouse pointer. Rather than executing the command, a helpful description of the command appears in a pop-up window.
	A description of a toolbar button	Point to a toolbar button to display its ToolTip label. You can also choose Help, What's This? from the Menu bar and then click a toolbar button to display more detailed help information in a pop-up window.

In this section, you access context-sensitive help.

Perform the following steps . . .

1. Let's practice choosing Help, What's This? to access Help for the File, New command and one of the toolbar buttons. Let's start with the File, New command.
   CHOOSE: Help

2. To activate the question mark mouse pointer:
   CHOOSE: What's This?

3. CHOOSE: File, New
   Rather than executing the command, Word provides a description of the command.

4. After reading the description, close the window by clicking on it once.

5. To display information about a toolbar button:
   CHOOSE: Help, What's This?
   CLICK: Open button (📂) on the Standard toolbar
   The following pop-up window appears:

> **Open (File menu)**
> Opens or finds a file.

6. CLICK: the pop-up window once to remove it

7. Word also provides a special Help tool called the Office Assistant. The Office Assistant watches your keystrokes as you work and offers suggestions and shortcuts. The Office Assistant may appear as a paperclip (by default) or as another character. At this point, if the Office Assistant already appears on your screen, as it does in Figure 1.7, skip to Step 8.
To display the Office Assistant:
CLICK: Office Assistant button (⬚)
The Office Assistant and its associated tip window appear. Your screen should appear similar to Figure 1.7.

FIGURE 1.7

OFFICE ASSISTANT AND
TIP WINDOW

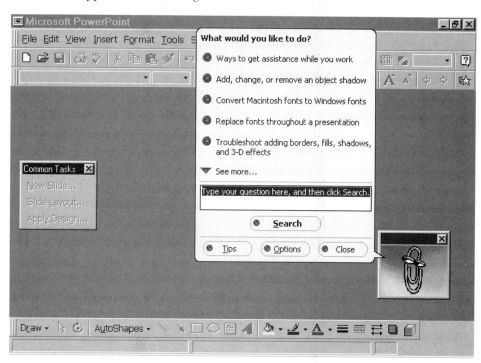

8. To type in a question about using clip art in a presentation:
TYPE: **use clip art**

9. To display information about your topic, click the Search button.
CLICK: Search button in the tip window
A list of related topics appears.

10. To close the tip window:
CLICK: Close button
The Office Assistant box, without the tip window, now appears in the presentation window. By simply clicking the animated character, the Office Assistant will display information about the procedure you are performing. Occasionally an illuminated light bulb will appear in the Office Assistant box. This is the Office Assistant's way of telling you it has a new tip or suggestion. You tell the Office Assistant that you want to view the tip by clicking the light bulb.

11. To remove the Office Assistant:
CLICK: Close button (☒) in its top right-hand corner

QUICK REFERENCE
Displaying Context-
Sensitive Help
	1. **CHOOSE: Help, What's This?**
	2. **Using the question mark mouse pointer, select the desired item for which you want to display a help pop-up window:**
	   • **CHOOSE: a menu command, or**
	   • **CLICK: a toolbar button, or**
	   • **CLICK: a dialog box item**

IN ADDITION CUSTOMIZING THE OFFICE ASSISTANT

To customize the Office Assistant, you do the following:

1. Ensure that the Office Assistant box appears.

2. RIGHT-CLICK: the Office Assistant character in the box

3. CHOOSE: Choose Assistant from the menu

4. Use the Gallery tab to select your favorite Office Assistant.

5. Select or remove features in the Options tab.

6. When finished, press (ENTER) or CLICK: OK

HELP TOPICS WINDOW

The primary way that you access PowerPoint's Help system is by choosing the Help, Contents and Index command from the menu. This command displays the Help Topics window, as shown in Figure 1.8. You can think of the Help Topics window as the front door to PowerPoint's vast help resources.

FIGURE 1.8

HELP TOPICS WINDOW:
CONTENTS TAB

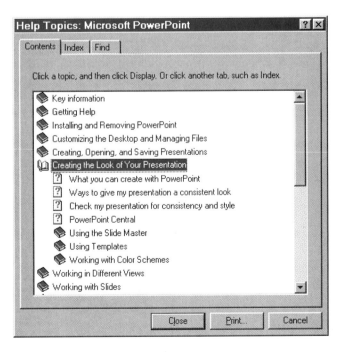

The Help Topics window provides three different tools, each on its own tab, to help you find the information you need quickly and easily. You point to and click a tab using the mouse to make the tab active in the window. Refer to the following tab descriptions to determine which tool you should use when requiring assistance:

- *Contents* tab   Displays a list of help topics organized as a hierarchy of books and pages. Think of this tab as the Table of Contents for the entire Help system. You navigate through categories by double-clicking book icons (📘) until reaching the desired help topic (?). Notice in Figure 1.8 that there are three different types of icons displayed:

    📘   represents a help category; double-click a book icon to view the books and topics it contains

    📖   represents an open category that is currently displaying its contents; double-click an open book icon to close (or collapse) the book

    ?   represents a help topic; double-click a topic icon to display a help window

- *Index* tab   Displays an alphabetical list of keywords and phrases, similar to a traditional book index. To search for a topic using this tab, you type a word (or even a few letters) into the text box which, in turn, makes the list box scroll to the first matching entry in the index. When the desired entry appears in the list box, double-click it to display the help topic. If a keyword has more than one associated topic, a Topics Found window appears and you can select a further topic to narrow your search.

- *Find* tab   Provides the ability to conduct a full-text search of the Help system for finding a particular word or phrase. Although similar to the *Index* tab, this tab differs in its ability to look past indexed keywords and search the help text itself.

When you double-click a help topic, it is displayed in a *secondary* window. You may find that secondary windows include some unfamiliar buttons, like ⏭️ and ◀️, embedded in the help text. The ⏭️ symbol, which we'll call the Chiclet button, represents a "See Also" link that you can click to move to a related help topic. The ◀️ symbol, called the Show Me button, initiates the command you're interested in. You may also notice that some words or phrases in the help window have a dotted underline. If you click such a word or phrase, a definition pop-up window appears.

In this section, you access the Help Topics window.

Perform the following steps . . .

1. CHOOSE: Help, Contents and Index

2. CLICK: *Contents* tab
   Your screen should now appear similar to Figure 1.8, except that your book categories will appear collapsed. (*Note*: The Help Topics window remembers the tab that was selected when it was last closed. It will automatically return to this tab the next time you access the Help system. For example, if you close the Help Topics window with the *Index* tab active, it will appear active the next time you display the window.)

3. To display the contents of a book:
   DOUBLE-CLICK: "📘 Creating the Look of Your Presentation" book
   (*Note*: You can double-click the book icon (📘) or the book's title. If you find it difficult to double-click using the mouse, you can also select or highlight the book by clicking it once and then click the Open command button.) This particular book contains four topic pages and three additional book categories.

4. To further clarify the search:
   DOUBLE-CLICK: "📘 Using Templates" book
   Notice that this book contains three topics.

5. To display a help topic:
   DOUBLE-CLICK: "❓ Create my own template" topic
   The Help Topics window is removed from view and a secondary window appears with the topic information.

6. To print the help topic:
   RIGHT-CLICK: anywhere in the help text of the secondary window
   CHOOSE: Print Topic (as shown in Figure 1.9)
   (*Note*: You can also print help information directly from the *Contents* tab. If you select a book by clicking on it once and then click the Print command button, the entire book—including the additional book categories that may be contained within the book—is sent to the printer. If you select an individual topic and click Print in the Help Topics window, only the highlighted topic is sent to the printer.)

FIGURE 1.9

DISPLAYING A HELP
TOPIC AND A SHORTCUT
MENU

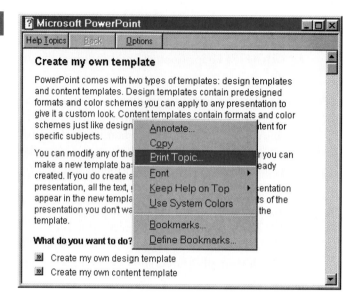

7. In the Print dialog box that appears:

- CLICK: OK command button to print the topic, or

- CLICK: Cancel command button if you do not have a printer

Whatever your selection, you are returned to the secondary window. (*Note*: If you selected to print the topic and your computer does not have a printer connected, you may be returned to Word with an error message. In this case, choose Help, Contents and Index to redisplay the Help Topics window and then proceed to Step 10.)

8. To close the secondary window and return to the Help Topics window: CLICK: Help Topics button (immediately under the Title bar)

9. To close the current book:
DOUBLE-CLICK: "📖 Creating the Look of Your Presentation" book
Notice that the list of books and topics is collapsed under the book icon.

10. Let's search for some information using the keyword index:
CLICK: *Index* tab

11. To find the topics related to Word's AutoFormat feature:
TYPE: `autoclipart`
The list automatically scrolls to the "AutoClipArt command" topic.

12. To display a sub-topic located beneath one of the "AutoClipArt command" headings:
DOUBLE-CLICK: AutoClipArt command
A secondary window appears with a few related topics.

13. DOUBLE-CLICK: "Ways to insert pictures in a presentation" topic

14. Since this window contains so much information, let's maximize it to fill the presentation window.
CLICK: Maximize button (🔲) in the secondary window

15. You may have noticed that a term in this secondary window appears with a dotted underline. To view the definition of this term, do the following:
CLICK: "bitmaps" with the hand mouse pointer (🖑)
A pop-up window appears with a definition.

16. After reading the help text, remove the definition pop-up window:
CLICK: the pop-up window once

17. To return to the Help Topics window:
CLICK: Help Topics button

18. Let's close the Microsoft Word Help system. To do so:
CLICK: Cancel command button (in the lower right-hand corner)
The Help Topics window is removed. (*Remember*: The next time you open the Help Topics window, the *Index* tab will be selected.)

QUICK REFERENCE	
QUICK REFERENCE Searching for Help Using the Help Topics Window	**1.** **To display the Help Topics window:** **CHOOSE: Help, Contents and Index** **2.** **CLICK:** *Contents* **tab to navigate a hierarchical Help system** **CLICK:** *Index* **tab to search for a word or phrase in a keyword index** **CLICK:** *Find* **tab to conduct a full-text search of the Help system**

OPENING A PRESENTATION

In this section, you open a presentation that we've created for you. You will find this presentation file at your *Advantage Files location*. In this learning guide, we refer to the following two locations when saving and opening files:

- *Advantage Files location*—This location may be on a diskette, in a folder on your local hard drive, or in a folder on a network server. The Advantage Files are the presentation files that have been created for you and that you will retrieve in the remaining exercises in this guide.

- *Data Files location*—This location may also be on a diskette, in a hard drive folder, or in a network folder. You will save the presentations that you create or modify to the Data Files location. This location may be the same disk or folder where you keep the Advantage Files; however **if you are using diskettes we recommend you keep the Advantage Files and Data Files on separate diskettes.** Otherwise, you will run out of storage space.

> **IMPORTANT:** *Before continuing, ensure that you know the location of your Advantage Files and where to store your Data Files. If necessary, ask your instructor or lab assistant for additional information.*

When opening a presentation, your first step is to display the Open dialog box by clicking the Open button (📂) on the Standard toolbar or choosing File, Open from the Menu bar. Once the Open dialog box appears, you select where the file is stored by clicking in the *Look in* drop-down list box and then selecting a file location. To load the presentation, you double-click the file's name appearing in the file list.

Next you open a file from your Advantage Files location.

Perform the following steps . . .

1. Make sure you have identified the location for retrieving the Advantage Files. If you require a diskette, place it into the diskette drive now.

2. To practice using the Open dialog box:
   CLICK: Open button (📂) on the Standard toolbar

3. To view the Advantage Files:
   CLICK: down arrow beside the *Look in* drop-down list box
   SELECT: *your Advantage Files location*
   The Open dialog box should now appear similar to Figure 1.10.

   Note: In this guide, we save presentations to the "My Documents" folder on the hard disk and retrieve presentations from the "PPT97" sub-folder, which is located at the following path:
   \My Documents\Advantage\PPT97

FIGURE 1.10

THE OPEN DIALOG BOX

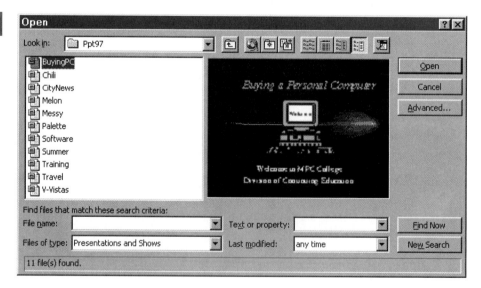

4. To change the display in the Open dialog box, try the following:
   CLICK: Detail button (▦) to see each presentation's file size and date
   CLICK: Properties button (▦) to see summary information
   CLICK: Preview button (▦) to see a presentation preview
   CLICK: List button (▦) to see a multiple-column format

5. Let's open a presentation:
DOUBLE-CLICK: BuyingPC
The presentation is loaded into PowerPoint's presentation window. Your screen now should now appear similar to Figure 1.11.

FIGURE 1.11

THE "BUYINGPC"
PRESENTATION FILE

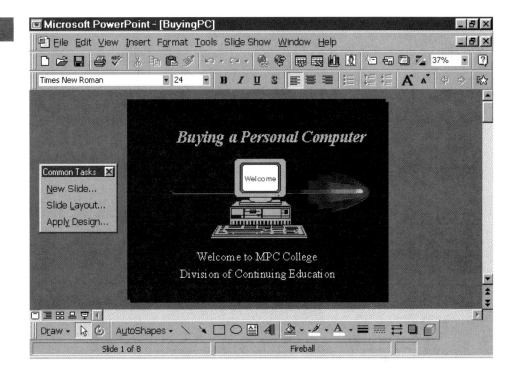

QUICK REFERENCE
Opening a Document

1. **CLICK: Open button (****), or**
   CHOOSE: File, Open from the Menu bar
2. **CLICK: down arrow beside the *Look in* drop-down list box**
3. **SELECT: a file location**
4. **DOUBLE-CLICK: the desired presentation**

IN ADDITION OPENING A PRESENTATION FROM THE WINDOWS DESKTOP

From the Windows desktop, you can open a presentation that you've worked with recently. Click the Start button on the taskbar and then choose the Documents command.

Then, choose the document's name. The application you used to create the document loads automatically.

VIEWING A PRESENTATION

PowerPoint provides five different views of a presentation: Slide view, Outline view, Slide Sorter view, Notes Page view, and Slide Show view. You switch among these views using the View command on the Menu bar or by clicking the View buttons located in the bottom left-hand corner of the presentation window. The active view of your presentation before being saved or closed becomes the default view when it is subsequently opened. Each view is described and illustrated in the following section.

SLIDE VIEW

The most common view to use for building or finalizing a presentation is Slide view. Similar to Page Layout view in Word for Windows, this view shows you how the slide will appear when printed or displayed. All text, graphics, and other media elements in your presentation appear in Slide view. You can perform the following tasks in Slide view:

- Insert, edit, and delete text
- Draw lines, squares, ovals, polygons, or other objects
- Add clip art, scanned photographs, or other media objects
- Add graphs, charts, or data from other applications
- Change the appearance of text and objects
- Change a template's style or color scheme

To select the Slide view, click the Slide view button (🖻) or choose View, Slides from the menu. There are three toolbars, by default, that are available in Slide view—Standard, Formatting, and Drawing. As mentioned previously, you can add or remove toolbars using the shortcut menu, accessed by clicking the right mouse button over any toolbar button.

OUTLINE VIEW

Outline view is especially useful for organizing your thoughts and developing the textual content for a presentation. You can also use Outline view much as you would a word processor to enter, arrange, and edit textual information. You perform the following tasks in Outline view:

- Insert, arrange, and edit textual content (titles and main body text)
- Promote and/or demote textual content in your outline
- Display a slide's text with or without formatting
- Show a slide's titles only, or show titles and full text

To select the Outline view, click the Outline view button () or choose View, Outline from the menu. In Outline view, the Outlining toolbar replaces the Drawing toolbar that is usually displayed in Slide view.

SLIDE SORTER VIEW

The Slide Sorter view provides a light table for viewing multiple slides. When selected, this view arranges thumbnail representations of your slides, complete with text and graphics, in rows and columns. Slide Sorter view gives you an immediate feeling for the continuity or flow of a presentation. You perform the following tasks in Slide Sorter view:

- Manipulate the order of slides
- Add transitional effects from one slide to another
- Incorporate special "build effects" for a particular slide, such as highlighting each point in turn
- Hide slides from being displayed in a computer-based slide show
- Set timing options for rehearsing your presentation

To select the Slide Sorter view, click the Slide Sorter view button () or choose View, Slide Sorter from the menu. In Slide Sorter view, the Slide Sorter toolbar replaces the Formatting toolbar.

NOTES PAGE VIEW

The Notes Page view allows you to insert, edit, and delete reminder notes for yourself on each slide. You can also use a slide's notes page for creating extended notes as an audience handout. Whatever the purpose, this view lets you enter text and graphics in a Notes placeholder located below the image of the slide.

To select the Notes Page view, click the Notes Page view button () or choose View, Notes Page from the menu.

SLIDE SHOW VIEW

In Slide Show view, the presentation is displayed as an electronic computer-based slide show, complete with slide transitions and timing effects. The ability to switch quickly among the different views allows you to modify a slide's content in Slide or Outline view and receive immediate feedback in Slide Show view. This view is also called an *on-screen presentation*.

To select the Slide Show view, click the Slide Show view button ( ) or choose View, Slide Show from the menu. The most common methods for controlling a presentation in Slide Show view appear in Table 1.3.

TABLE 1.3	*Task Description*	*Keyboard and Mouse Methods*
Controlling a Slide Show Presentation	Go to the next slide	CLICK: left mouse button, or PRESS: PgDn, ➡, ⬇, ENTER, Spacebar, or TYPE: N
	Go to the previous slide	PRESS: PgUp, ⬅, ⬆, or TYPE: P
	Go to a specific slide	TYPE: desired slide number, and then PRESS: ENTER
	Go to the first slide	PRESS: HOME
	Blank the screen to black	PRESS: b to blank screen to black PRESS: b again to unblank screen
	Blank the screen to white	PRESS: w to blank screen to white PRESS: w again to unblank screen
	Exit the slide show	PRESS: ESC

If you click the right mouse button in Slide Show view, a shortcut menu appears that provides options that are similar to those described in Table 1.3.

FOR PRACTICE

Let's practice switching among the views using the "BuyingPC" presentation.

Perform the following steps . . .

1. First, let's remove the Common Tasks toolbar from view.
   RIGHT-CLICK: Common Tasks toolbar
   CHOOSE: Common Tasks

2. To display the "BuyingPC" presentation in Outline view:
   CLICK: Outline View button ( )
   Your screen should now appear similar to Figure 1.12.

FIGURE 1.12

OUTLINE VIEW

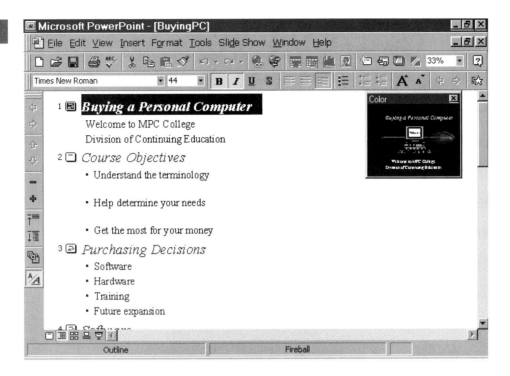

3. To display the "BuyingPC" presentation in Slide Sorter view:
CLICK: Slide Sorter view button (▣)
Your screen should now appear similar to Figure 1.13.

FIGURE 1.13

SLIDE SORTER VIEW

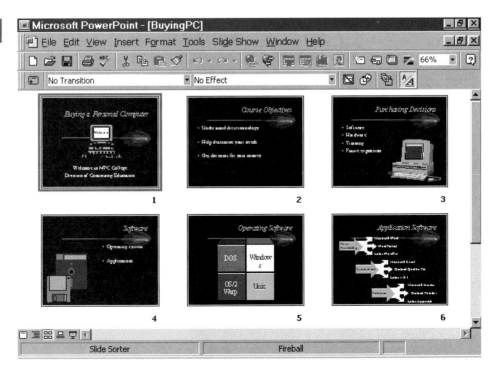

4. To display the presentation in Notes Page view:
CLICK: Notes Page view button (▣)
Your screen should now appear similar to Figure 1.14.

FIGURE 1.14

NOTES PAGE VIEW

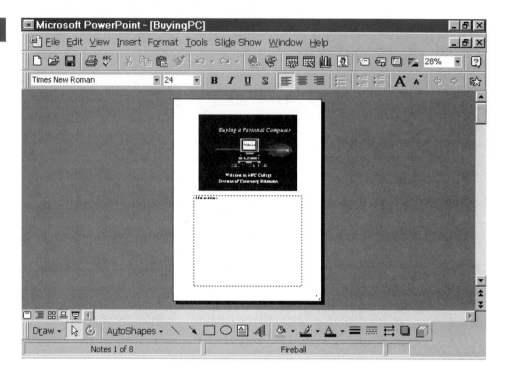

5. To display the presentation in Slide Show view:
CLICK: Slide Show view button (▣)
Your screen should now appear similar to Figure 1.15.

FIGURE 1.15

SLIDE SHOW VIEW

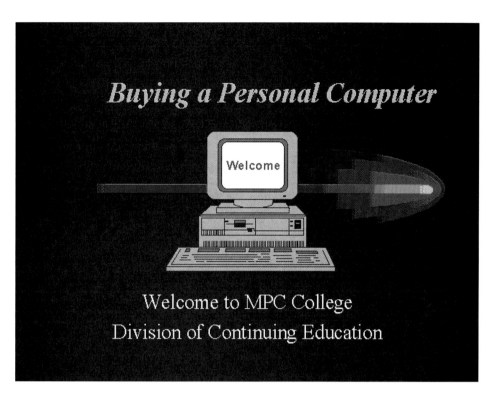

6. To proceed to the next slide in the presentation:
   CLICK: left mouse button once

7. To display the next slide using the keyboard:
   PRESS: Spacebar

8. To return to the previous slide using the keyboard:
   PRESS: ⬆

9. To return to the first slide in the presentation:
   PRESS: (HOME)

10. To exit the Slide Show view:
    PRESS: (ESC)

11. Return to Slide view.
    CLICK: Slide view button ([▣])

12. Before continuing to the next section, redisplay the Common Tasks toolbar.
    RIGHT-CLICK: the Standard toolbar
    CHOOSE: Common Tasks

QUICK REFERENCE
Changing the View
for a Presentation

- CLICK: [▯] to change to Slide view
- CLICK: [☰] to change to Outline view
- CLICK: [▦] to change to Slide Sorter view
- CLICK: [▣] to change to Notes Page view
- CLICK: [▽] to change to Slide Show view

- **CLICK:** left mouse button to go to the next slide
- **CLICK:** right mouse button to go to the previous slide
- **TWIN-CLICK:** left and right mouse buttons and hold for two seconds to go to first slide
- **PRESS:** ESC to exit Slide Show view

CLOSING A PRESENTATION

When you are finished working with a presentation, you should close the file to free up valuable computer memory. To close a presentation window, choose File, Close from the Menu bar or click the Close icon (☒) in the presentation window. If you've made changes to your presentation since you last saved it, you should save the presentation before you close the window.

Let's now close the "BuyingPC" presentation.

Perform the following steps . . .

1. Since you haven't made any changes to the presentation:
   CHOOSE: File, Close

2. If there are any other presentations appearing in the slide area, repeat Step 1 to clear them from memory.

- **CHOOSE: File, Close, or**
- **CLICK: Close icon (☒) of the Presentation window**

LEAVING POWERPOINT

When you are finished using PowerPoint, save your work and exit the program by clicking the Close button (☒) that is located in the Title bar of the application window or choose File, Exit from the Menu bar. If you have made modifications to the presentation and have not saved the changes, PowerPoint asks whether the presentation should be saved or abandoned before exiting the program.

Now you will end the current working session.

Perform the following steps . . .

1. CLICK: Close button (☒) of the application window
   Assuming that no changes were made to the document, the application is closed and you are returned to the Windows desktop.

2. To exit Windows:
   CHOOSE: Start, Shut Down
   SELECT: *Shutdown the computer?* option button
   CLICK: Yes command button

QUICK REFERENCE	• CLICK: Close button (☒) of the application window, or
Exiting PowerPoint	• CHOOSE: File, Exit

Summary

PowerPoint provides you with powerful tools for creating presentations. A presentation can include one or more of the following: slides, handouts, speaker's notes, and outlines. In this session, after loading Microsoft Windows and PowerPoint, you were led on a guided tour of the program's major components. We also used the Help facility to retrieve information on menu commands and toolbar buttons.

Near the end of the session, you opened an existing presentation and practiced using the View buttons—located at the bottom of the presentation window—to display the presentation in five different views. These views included Slide view, Outline view, Slide Sorter view, Notes Pages view, and Slide Show view. The session concluded when you closed the presentation and exited PowerPoint.

COMMAND SUMMARY

Many of the commands and procedures appearing in this session are provided in Table 1.4 below.

TABLE 1.4	Task Description	Menu Command	Alternative Method
Command Summary	Access the PowerPoint Help facility	Help, Contents and Index	
	Access the Office Assistant	Help, Microsoft PowerPoint Help	☐
	Access context-sensitive descriptions	Help, What's This?	
	Open an existing presentation file	File, Open	☐
	Close a presentation file	File, Close	☒
	Leave PowerPoint	File, Exit	☒

Key Terms

application window
In Microsoft Windows, each running application program appears in its own application window. These windows can be sized and moved anywhere on the Windows desktop.

handout

In PowerPoint, a handout which is given to audience members with two to six small images of the actual slides on each printed page.

hyperlinks

Highlighted words or phrases that appear when viewing information on the World Wide Web. You click the hyperlink to view a different document.

Internet

A collection of computer networks that spans the globe.

Intranet

A local or wide area network that uses Internet technologies to share information.

presentation

In PowerPoint, a presentation is a collection of slides, handouts, speaker's notes, and outlines, all in one disk file.

presentation window

In PowerPoint, each open presentation appears in its own presentation window. These windows can be sized and moved anywhere within the Slide work area. (A presentation window represents your workspace.)

run-time version

A scaled-down version of the original software that includes a "player" for the application's data files, but does not usually allow the user access to any editing features.

slide

In PowerPoint, a slide is an individual page of a presentation.

template

A template defines how slide text will look, where the text and other objects will be positioned, and what colors will be used.

wizards

Wizards lead you through creating presentations and performing other tasks in PowerPoint.

World Wide Web (WWW)

A visual interface for the Internet.

EXERCISES

SHORT ANSWER

1. What does the term *integration* mean as it relates to Microsoft Office?

2. What is the purpose of *PowerPoint Central*?

3. What are some of the output options for a presentation?

4. What is a dialog box?

5. How do you display the Help Topics window?

6. How do you open a presentation?

7. Describe the five different views that are available in PowerPoint.

8. In Slide Show view, how do you proceed to the next slide?

9. In Slide Show view, how do you return to the previous slide?

10. In Slide Show view, how do you return to the first slide?

HANDS-ON

(*Note*: Ensure that you know the location of your Advantage Files and where to store your Data Files. If necessary, ask your instructor or lab assistant for additional information.)

1. In this exercise, you practice accessing PowerPoint's Help facility.

   a. Load Microsoft PowerPoint.

   b. Remove the PowerPoint dialog box when it appears.

   c. Using the Help, What's This? command, retrieve help for the Open button (⊞).

   d. After reading the contents of the Help window, close the window.

   e. In the Help Topics window, display the *Index* tab.

   f. Search for information on "opening presentations."

   g. Display the *Contents* tab.

   h. Browse through the Help topics by pressing the ⬇ key repeatedly.

   i. Close the Help Topics window.

   j. Using the Office Assistant, display help for "using color in presentations."

   k. Close the Office Assistant and tip window before proceeding.

2. In this exercise, you open the presentation named "Training" from the Advantage Files location.

   a. Open the "Training" presentation from the Advantage Files location.

   b. If the presentation isn't maximized in the presentation window, click its Maximize button (▣).

   c. Display the presentation in Slide Sorter view.

   d. Display the presentation in Outline view.

   e. Display the presentation in Notes Page view.

   f. Display the presentation in Slide Show view.

   g. Let the slide show run on its own. (*Note*: You don't have to click the mouse button to display the next slide because transitions have been built into this presentation.) If you need to exit from the presentation before you've viewed all the slides, press ESC.

   h. Close the "Training" presentation.

3. In this exercise, you open the presentation named "Summer" from the Advantage Files location.

   a. Open the "Summer" presentation from the Advantage Files location.

   b. Display the presentation in Slide Show view.

   c. Practice navigating through the presentation using the keyboard and mouse methods.

   d. Move directly to slide number 3.

   e. Display the first slide in the presentation.

   f. Blank the presentation to a black screen.

   g. Unhide the presentation.

   h. Blank the presentation to a white screen.

   i. Unhide the presentation.

   j. Return to Slide view.

   k. Close the "Summer" presentation.

4. On your own, learn more about giving presentations by reviewing one of PowerPoint's presentations. To begin, choose File, New from the Menu bar and then click the *Presentations* tab. Then double-click the "Presentation Guidelines-Dale Carnegie Training" presentation template. (*Note*: You must click the template name to see its full name.) Display the presentation in Slide view and review its contents. When you're finished, close the presentation.

CASE PROBLEMS   **VACATION VISTAS, INC.**

(*Note*: In the following case problems, assume the role of the primary characters and perform the same steps that they identify. You may want to re-read the session opening.)

1. Frank stares intently at the opened courier package in front of him. The letter from Juanita, which he has already read and is still digesting, has been placed neatly upon his desk. He now reads the sticky note in his left hand. *Frank, the presentation file at the Advantage Files location is called "V-Vistas." I recommend that you proof the textual and graphical content in the presentation. Bye for now, Juanita.*

   Not one to waste too much time sulking, Frank plans his approach. He loads the presentation into PowerPoint and gets an overall feel for the product using the Slide Sorter view. To proof the textual content, Frank switches to Outline view and finds two blatant mistakes. He writes down the two mistakes on a notepad that will later become his review letter to Juanita. To proof the graphical content, Frank uses the Slide view and again finds two obvious mistakes in the graphics that Juanita chose for the presentation. As before, Frank copies down the two mistakes on his note pad.

Having closed the presentation, Frank must now write a letter to Juanita Gomez specifying the two textual errors and the two graphical errors in the "V-Vistas" presentation. He addresses it to her Seattle home at 1500 Country Club Lane, Seattle WA 98004. He'll include this review letter when he sends the disk back to Juanita for final production.

2. With only one week to go before his presentation at the local seniors' hall, Frank is getting a little nervous. As the expected attendance exceeds 100 seniors, he has rented a speaker's podium, a 35 mm slide projector, and a large screen. Unfortunately, Frank isn't used to speaking in front of large groups and truly wanted some time to practice before the actual presentation.

    Having learned the fundamentals of PowerPoint, Frank remembers that he can use the Slide Show view to display and work through the presentation. He loads the "V-Vistas" presentation into PowerPoint and switches to Slide Show view. After progressing through four slides, Frank notices one of his staff passing by his office door with a client. Not wanting the client to see the unfinished presentation, Frank blanks the screen to black temporarily. When he unhides the presentation, he backs up a couple of slides to refocus his attention. With his train of thought interrupted, he decides to return to the first slide and start again. This time, he makes it all the way through the presentation.

3. Having finished practicing, Frank decides to close the "V-Vistas" presentation file and exit Microsoft PowerPoint. He doesn't save any changes that he may have made in the presentation. Before leaving his office for the evening, Frank writes down a summary of the five views and the primary methods for navigating a presentation in Slide Show view. He places the summary beside his monitor for easy reference.

Microsoft PowerPoint 97 for Windows

Creating a Presentation

SESSION OUTLINE

INTRODUCTION

Compare electronic slide presentations with hand-written or typed overheads and you can immediately appreciate the value and impact of using presentation software like PowerPoint. But not only are electronic presentations more effec-tive, they can take less time and effort to create. In this session, you learn how to improve the quality of your presentations while dramatically reducing your production timelines and budgets.

BERKFORD COLLEGE, PENNSYLVANIA

Sharon Rheingold is a second-year law student at Berkford College in Pennsylvania. As a credit component toward her studies this semester, Sharon accepted a job teaching Public Speaking 101 to first-year business students. Given her goal of one day becoming a successful trial lawyer, Sharon saw this job as an opportunity to hone her communication skills on a captive audience. Little did she realize that Dr. Kirsten Antoski, the dean of Business Administration, had personally developed the course and expects each of her instructors to hand out professional presentation materials for each lecture. With an already suffocating course load, Sharon wonders how she can possibly meet Dr. Antoski's expectations and complete her own studies.

While discussing the situation with her roommate Walt, the two students thought of an especially good idea. Walt, a fourth-year student in the Faculty of Education, recommended Sharon use Microsoft PowerPoint to develop her lesson plans and course notes. Walt assured Sharon that with only a few tips she would be producing professional-looking handouts in hours instead of days. Furthermore, she could use PowerPoint to help teach her students some of the principles of public speaking.

In this session, you and Sharon learn how to use the AutoContent Wizard to create new presentations quickly and easily. You also learn how to use a design template, modify a slide's information, save a presentation to the disk, and print a presentation.

CREATING A PRESENTATION: AN OVERVIEW

Even if you haven't had much experience using PowerPoint, creating a new presentation is easy. You'll be amazed at how quickly you can organize content, select an output medium, and design the look of your slides. Though you may initially believe otherwise, the most time-consuming task involves gathering and writing the content for a presentation. It is important that you have a clear understanding of a presentation's objectives and can verbalize the information that you want to communicate to an audience. Anybody can choose background colors, apply fonts and styles, and insert graphics on a slide. Your goal is to create a presentation that communicates a message effectively—and that takes work.

USING POWERPOINT TO CREATE A PRESENTATION

The following steps provide an overview of the process for creating a presentation using Microsoft PowerPoint:

1. *Select a starting point for your presentation.*
   In the startup dialog box (Figure 2.1) that appears when you first load PowerPoint, the *AutoContent Wizard* and *Template* options can help you get started creating a new presentation. The **AutoContent Wizard** provides the quickest and easiest method for creating a presentation by presenting you with a series of questions about the subject, type of output for your presentation, and presentation style. If you just want to pick a subject or a visual style for a presentation, choose the *Template* option. For the greatest flexibility, you can create a presentation from scratch using the *Blank Presentation* option.

FIGURE 2.1

THE POWERPOINT
STARTUP DIALOG BOX

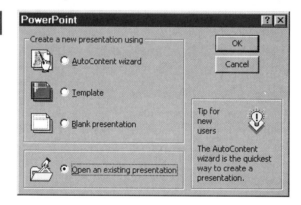

2. *Create the individual slides for your presentation.*
   After you select the starting point for your slide presentation, you must create the individual slides by adding, editing, and deleting text and graphics for each slide page. You typically use the Outline view to enter a slide's textual content and the Slide view to finalize the colors, typefaces, and placement of graphics, charts, and other objects. If you started creating a presentation using the AutoContent Wizard or by picking a presentation template, many of the slides for your presentation are automatically added to the presentation file. You simply edit the titles and body text on the slides to ensure their appropriateness for the topic. When you create a blank presentation, PowerPoint provides you with the first slide; you must create any additional slides from scratch.

3. Review and refine your presentation in its entirety.
   Once you've created the individual slides, you use Slide Sorter view and Slide Show view to review the presentation. While working in Slide Sorter view, you can manipulate the linear order of the slides, set the timing for rehearsing a presentation, hide slides, and add special effects to your presentation. For example, PowerPoint provides you with the ability to create **build slides** for computer-based presentations. On a build slide, you can make bullets appear on the screen one at a time and even dim previous points on the slide to draw further attention to the current bullet. Also, in Slide Sorter view you can incorporate transitions into your presentation. A **transition** is the visual effect you see when you go from one slide to the next in a computer-based presentation. For the acid test of previewing your work as it would be presented live, you use the Slide Show view.

4. *Save and print your presentation.*
   Not to tempt fate, you should save your presentation regularly as you work. Also, print your presentation for others to review. It's always wise to let your friends and co-workers find the errors before your audience has the opportunity! A second benefit of printing a presentation is that you will have a paper copy in case your computer files are deleted accidentally or become corrupted by a virus.

REACHING FOR THE DICTIONARY

Before you create a presentation in the next section, let's introduce and define some important terms:

Object

Your slides will typically contain one or more different elements, or objects. An object can be text, a graphic, a picture, a shape, and so on.

Design Template

Defined briefly in the last session, a design template is a presentation whose background, color scheme, typefaces, and other formatting options can be applied to another presentation. By using templates, you need not reinvent the wheel each time you create a presentation. PowerPoint provides 17 professionally designed templates from which you can choose. You can also design your own custom templates, using your corporate or school colors, for example, and then apply them to the new presentations you create.

Presentation Template

A presentation template is a presentation whose subject outline can be applied to another presentation. PowerPoint provides over 32 presentation templates that you can choose from to match your subject.

Default presentation format

PowerPoint provides a default presentation format—complete with a background design, color scheme, typefaces, and so on—that is applied when you choose the *Blank Presentation* option from the startup dialog box.

Masters

Each presentation you create contains a master for each output option in the presentation; that is, one for slides, one for the outline, one for the notes pages, and one for the audience handouts. Whatever you place on a master page will print on each page in the presentation, whether a slide page or a notes page. For example, to have a graphic of your company or school logo appear on each slide in the presentation, you place it on the Slide Master.

These terms will be explained further in later sections, but now we move on to learning by doing rather than by reading!

USING THE AUTOCONTENT WIZARD

If you're finding it difficult to organize and write down your thoughts, select the *AutoContent Wizard* option button from the startup dialog box or after choosing File, New from the Menu bar. After progressing through six dialog boxes, you'll have a skeletal framework for building a complete presentation.

In this section, you practice using the AutoContent Wizard.

 **Perform the following steps . . .**

1. Make sure that you've loaded Microsoft PowerPoint and that you've identified the location for storing your Data Files. If you require a diskette, place it into the diskette drive now.

2. If the Office Assistant (shown at the right) appears:
CLICK: Close button (⊠) in its top right-hand corner

3. If the PowerPoint startup dialog box appears on your screen, do the following (otherwise, proceed to Step 4):
SELECT: *AutoContent Wizard* option button
PRESS: **ENTER** or CLICK: OK
Now proceed to Step 5.

4. If the startup dialog box does not appear on your screen and you are certain that Microsoft PowerPoint is loaded, do the following to initiate the AutoContent Wizard:
CHOOSE: File, New from the Menu bar
CLICK: *Presentations* tab
DOUBLE-CLICK: AutoContent Wizard icon

(*CAUTION*: A message may appear warning you that the wizard you are about to open may contain a *macro virus*. This is just a warning message and doesn't mean that a virus exists. Because a virus can harm your data and program files, ensure that the files you open come from reputable sources. If you don't want this message to display the next time you activate a wizard, clear the *Always ask before opening presentations with macros* check box. For now, click the Enable Macros button.)

5. The AutoContent Wizard is launched and presents the initial AutoContent Wizard screen. Your screen should now appear similar to Figure 2.2. On the left side of the dialog box, you see the steps the AutoContent Wizard will go through in order to format the final presentation. To skip to a particular step, you click its associated box. Otherwise, if you click Next, the next step will occur.

FIGURE 2.2

AUTOCONTENT WIZARD:
INITIAL SCREEN

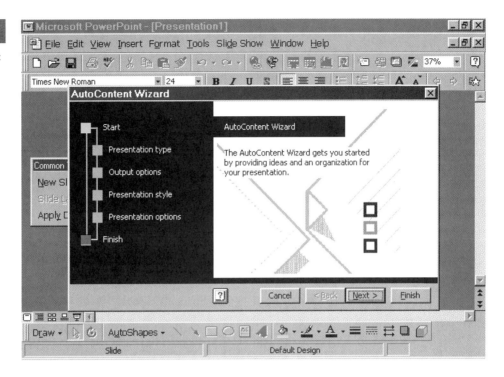

6. To proceed to the next screen (Presentation Type):
CLICK: Next button
Your screen should now appear similar to Figure 2.3.

FIGURE 2.3

AUTOCONTENT WIZARD:
CHOOSING THE TYPE
OF PRESENTATION

7. In this step you select the type of presentation you want to give. PowerPoint presents seven categories of presentations. When you click a category, a list of related presentations appears in the list box to the right. Make the following selections.
CLICK: Corporate button
SELECT: Company Meeting in the list box

8. To define the output options for the presentation.
CLICK: Next button

9. SELECT: *Presentations, informal meetings, handouts* option

10. To define the presentation style:
CLICK: Next button

11. Make the following selections.
SELECT: *On-screen presentation* option button
SELECT: No in the *Will you print handouts?* area

12. To proceed to the next screen:
CLICK: Next button

13. In this step, you enter the information you want to appear on the opening slide such as the title of your presentation, your name, and any personal information such as your company name. Use the mouse to move the cursor and to select text. (*Note:* You can also press `TAB` to move the cursor to the next text box and `SHIFT` + `TAB` to move to the previous text box.) After positioning the cursor, type the text you want to appear in the text box.

Before continuing to the next step:
SELECT: the text in the *Presentation title* text box, if necessary
TYPE: **Effective Communication Skills** in the *Presentation title* text box
SELECT: the text in the *Your name* text box, if necessary
TYPE: *your name* into the *Your name* text box
SELECT: the text in the *Additional information* text box, if necessary
TYPE: *your school or company name* into the *Additional information* text box
If you prefer fictitious information, refer to Figure 2.4.

FIGURE 2.4

AUTOCONTENT WIZARD:
CREATING THE TITLE
SLIDE

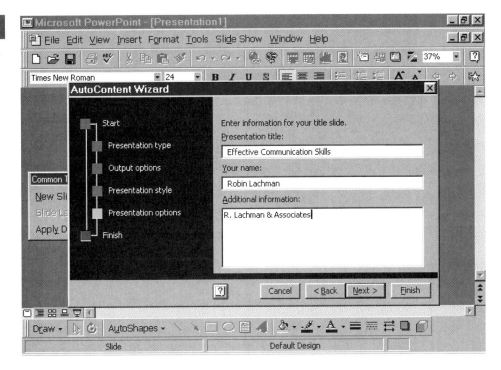

14. To continue:
CLICK: Next button

15. If you wish, review your selections by clicking the Back button. Otherwise:
CLICK: Finish button
The presentation is compiled and your presentation appears in Outline view (Figure 2.5). In this view, you see the text of your presentation and a slide miniature of the current slide. You can easily edit the text of your presentation in Outline view. We describe this view in more detail in Session 3.

FIGURE 2.5

YOUR PRESENTATION IN OUTLINE VIEW

16. To display the presentation in Slide Show view:
CLICK: Slide Show view button (▣)

17. To advance through the presentation:
CLICK: left mouse button continuously until you reach the end of the presentation and are returned to Outline view

18. Let's close the presentation and move on to the next section, where you will learn more about design templates. Do the following:
CHOOSE: File, Close
CLICK: No when asked whether you want to save the presentation

---

QUICK REFERENCE
Using the AutoContent Wizard

1. SELECT: *AutoContent Wizard* option button in the startup dialog box
PRESS: [ENTER] or CLICK: OK
(*Note:* You can also choose File, New and select the AutoContent Wizard from the *Presentations* tab.)

2. Proceed through the AutoContent Wizard dialog boxes, replying to questions and clicking the Next button.

3. When you reach the last slide:
CLICK: Finish button

IN ADDITION CREATE A PRESENTATION FOR USE ON THE WEB

1. CHOOSE: File, New from the Menu bar

2. CLICK: *Presentations* tab

3. SELECT: one of the "online" templates

4. Proceed by following the template's guidelines

USING A DESIGN TEMPLATE

One of the problems with the advent of presentation software like PowerPoint is that the presentation author has been hurled into the role of graphic designer. Many people who are highly skilled writers and content researchers find it difficult to take on the additional role of art director. Fortunately, PowerPoint provides 17 design templates to help those of us who consider themselves artistically challenged.

In this section, you create a presentation entitled "The Future of Computer and Communications Technology" for a class project. The objective of the presentation is to inform your classmates of three primary technology trends: connectivity, online information access, and interactivity.

Now you practice picking a design template.

Perform the following steps . . .

1. If the PowerPoint startup dialog box appears on your screen, click its Cancel button.

2. Your first step is to display the New Presentation dialog box:
CHOOSE: File, New

3. To select a design template:
CLICK: *Presentation Designs* tab

4. To view the design templates in a list:
CLICK: List button ( )
Your screen should now appear similar to Figure 2.6. (*Note*: You may not have the same design templates stored on your hard drive as those shown in Figure 2.6.)

FIGURE 2.6

NEW PRESENTATION
DIALOG BOX:
PRESENTATION
DESIGNS TAB

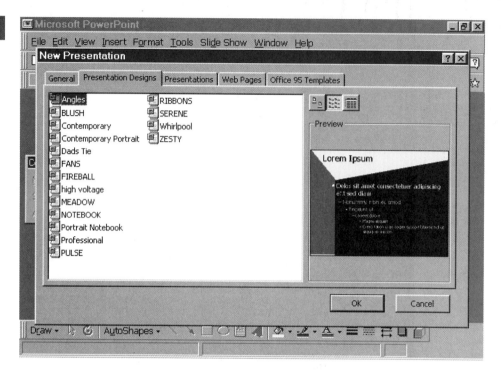

5. To preview a design template, you single-click the template name. An example of the design will appear in the Preview window. On your own, preview at least five design templates.

6. In this step, you will pick the "angles" design template:
    DOUBLE-CLICK: angles

7. PowerPoint needs to know what layout you want to use for the first slide (Figure 2.7). Notice that the name of the AutoLayout appears below the command buttons in the dialog box. Do the following:
    SELECT: Title Slide layout (located in the upper-left corner)
    PRESS: **ENTER** or CLICK: OK
    Your screen should now appear similar to Figure 2.8.

8. Before you modify this new presentation, let's continue to the next section to learn how to save it to disk.

FIGURE 2.7

NEW SLIDE DIALOG BOX

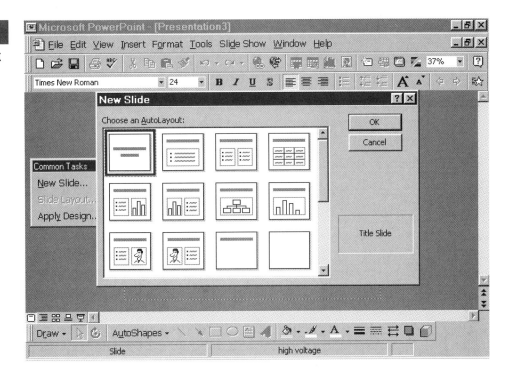

FIGURE 2.8

A TITLE SLIDE

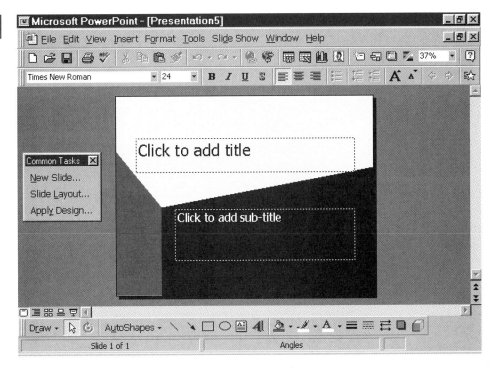

SAVING A PRESENTATION

When you work on a presentation, it exists only in the computer's RAM (random access memory) which is highly volatile. To permanently store your work, you must save the presentation to the hard disk, a network drive, or to a floppy diskette. Saving your work to a disk is similar to placing it into a filing cabinet. To be safe, you should save your work every 15 minutes, or whenever you're interrupted, to protect against an unexpected power outage or other catastrophe.

To save a presentation to a disk, you click the Save button (🖫) on the Standard toolbar or you select the File, Save command from the menu. If you haven't saved the presentation before, a dialog box appears where you specify the save location and name for the file. When naming a file, you can use up to 255 characters, including spaces. You can't use the following characters in filenames:

\   /   :   *   ?   "   <   > |

Now you will save the current presentation.

Perform the following steps . . .

1. Make sure that you have identified the location for storing your data files. If you require a diskette, place it into the diskette drive now.

2. CLICK: Save button (🖫)
   Your screen should now appear similar to Figure 2.9.

FIGURE 2.9

THE FILE SAVE DIALOG BOX

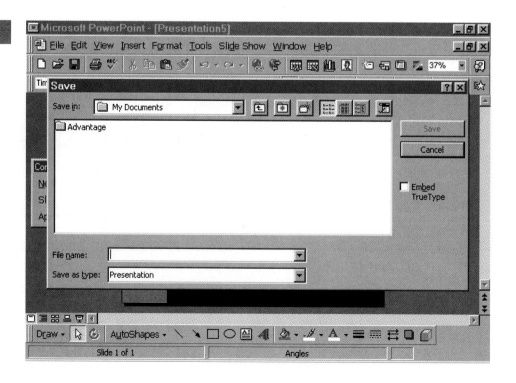

3. To specify a filename for the presentation:
TYPE: `Current Trends`

4. To specify where the presentation will be saved, do the following:
CLICK: down arrow beside the *Save in* drop-down list box
SELECT: *your Data Files location*
PRESS: [ENTER] or CLICK: Save command button

There are times when you'll want to save an existing presentation under a different filename. For example, you may want to keep different versions of the same presentation on your disk. Or, you may want to use one presentation as a template for future presentations that are similar in style and format. Rather than creating an entirely new presentation, you can retrieve an old presentation file, edit the information, and then save it under a different name using the File, Save As command. If you want to update or replace an existing file, you use File, Save or click the Save button (🖫).

QUICK REFERENCE
Saving a File

- **CLICK: Save button (🖫) on the Standard toolbar, or**
- **CHOOSE: File, Save, or**
- **CHOOSE: File, Save As to save a file under a different name**

IN ADDITION SAVE A PRESENTATION TO AN FTP SITE

If you want your presentation to be accessible to others on the Internet, consider saving it to an FTP site. *FTP (File Transfer Protocol)* makes it possible for users to transfer presentations over the Internet. You can save to an FTP site if your computer has an Internet connection that supports saving files. To save to an FTP site:

1. CHOOSE: File, Save As

2. SELECT: Internet Connections (FTP) from the Save in drop-down list

3. DOUBLE-CLICK: the site you want to save to (*Note:* You can add FTP sites to the list by selecting Add/Modify FTP Locations in the file area.)

4. TYPE: a name for your presentation

5. PRESS: [ENTER] or CLICK: Save command button

IN ADDITION SAVE AS HTML

To publish your PowerPoint presentation on the Web, you must save it in an HTML format first. *HTML (Hypertext Markup Language)* is a system for marking up documents so that they can be viewed on the World Wide Web. To save a presentation as an HTML document:

CHOOSE: File, Save as HTML

(*Note:* It is a good idea to choose File, Save to save your presentation in a PowerPoint format before saving it in an HTML file format. Then you can make changes to your presentation later.)

ADDING SLIDES

It's not just what you say, it's *how* you say it. As the old Chinese proverb has it, "Tell me and I'll forget; show me and I may remember; involve me and I'll understand." Involving an audience in your presentation means making it visually interesting, aesthetically pleasing, and relevant. Although we won't teach you writing skills in this guide, we will provide some pointers for communicating effectively using PowerPoint. To begin, your presentations should include some, if not all, of the following slides in addition to the body of the presentation:

- Use a *Title slide* to act as the backdrop for people entering the room or auditorium at the beginning of your presentation

- Use an *Introduction slide* to set the stage for your presentation and convince the audience that it will be a worthwhile use of their time

- Use an *Agenda* or *Objectives slide* to prepare the audience for what's coming up ahead in the presentation

- Use a *Closing slide* to reiterate and summarize your main ideas, to draw conclusions, and to revisit the presentation's objectives

Now that the "look" is defined for your presentation, let's create some slides. It's very easy; the instructions are right on the slide! As you proceed, you'll see that PowerPoint automatically creates **placeholders** on new slides for your text and graphics. There are three primary types of placeholders: Title or Sub-title, Text, and Object. While the first two are self-explanatory, an Object placeholder contains such items as clip art, graphs, and organizational charts. To edit a Title or Text placeholder, you click the mouse once in the placeholder and then type the desired text. To edit an Object placeholder, you double-click the mouse in the placeholder and create or pick the desired object.

When you add a new slide to your presentation, PowerPoint displays a dialog box with several **AutoLayout** options that are formats for positioning text and graphics using placeholders. These AutoLayouts include slide formats for title slides, bulleted lists, graphs, two-column text slides, tables, and slides with clip art or graphics. AutoLayouts provide a great starting point for creating new slides in your presentation.

ADDING TEXT TO A SLIDE

The slides you create in this section contain text only. You will edit the layout of the slides so that you can add graphics later in the session. In this section, you create the first two slides in the "Current Trends" presentation.

Perform the following steps . . .

1. Position the mouse pointer over the Title placeholder (appearing as "Click to add title" on the slide) and click the left mouse button once.

2. TYPE: CURRENT TRENDS IN COMPUTER TECHNOLOGY
   Notice that the text automatically wraps to the next line in the placeholder box. Do not press (ENTER) when you are finished typing.

3. CLICK: the Sub-title placeholder (appearing as "Click to add sub-title" on the slide)
   PRESS: (ENTER) to begin typing on the second line
   TYPE: by
   PRESS: (ENTER)
   TYPE: *your name*
   Notice that "Slide 1 of 1" appears in the Status bar. Your screen should now appear similar to Figure 2.10.

FIGURE 2.10

SLIDE 1 IN THE "CURRENT TRENDS" PRESENTATION

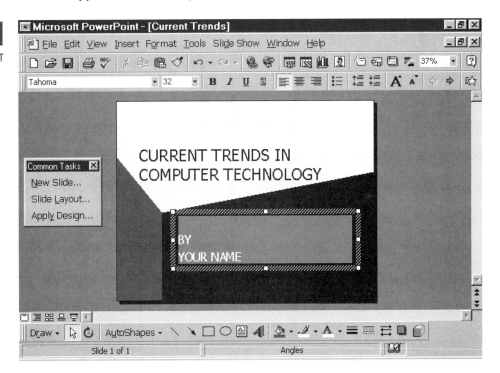

4. Let's add a second slide to the presentation. The easiest way to add a new slide is to use the Common Tasks toolbar, shown to the right. If the Common Tasks toolbar already appears in your application window, proceed with Step 5.

   Otherwise, point to an existing toolbar and then:
   RIGHT-CLICK: to display the shortcut menu
   CHOOSE: Common Tasks
   The Common Tasks toolbar should appear on your screen.

5. To add a new slide:
CHOOSE: New Slide from the Common Tasks toolbar
PowerPoint adds the new slide immediately following the currently active slide.

6. The New Slide dialog box appears, showing you the AutoLayout options for creating a new slide.
SELECT: Bulleted List
(*Note*: The Bulleted List may already be selected.)
PRESS: (ENTER) or CLICK: OK
Your screen should now appear similar to Figure 2.11. A new slide with a Title placeholder and a Text placeholder (appearing as "Click to add text" on the slide) is displayed in the presentation window. These placeholders correspond to the AutoLayout option that you just selected.

FIGURE 2.11

SLIDE 2 IN THE "CURRENT TRENDS" PRESENTATION

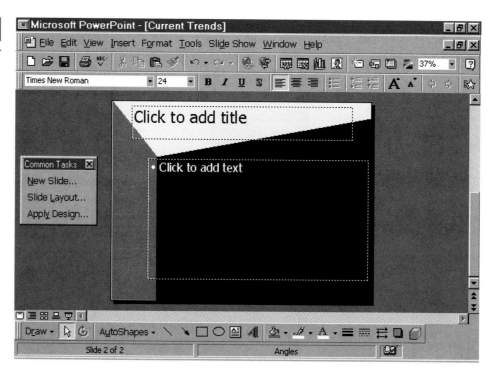

7. To add a title to the slide:
CLICK: Title placeholder
TYPE: The Leading Trends

8. To add content to the slide:
CLICK: Text placeholder
TYPE: Connectivity
PRESS: (ENTER)
TYPE: Interactivity
Your screen should now appear similar to Figure 2.12.

FIGURE 2.12

SLIDE 2: TEXT HAS BEEN
ENTERED

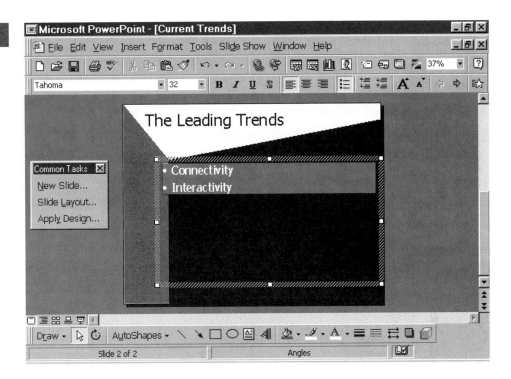

QUICK REFERENCE
Creating a Slide with Text

1. **To create a new slide:**

   CHOOSE: New Slide from the Common Tasks toolbar

   SELECT: an AutoLayout option in the New Slide dialog box

   PRESS: ENTER or CLICK: OK

2. **CLICK: a Title or Text placeholder in the slide**

   TYPE: *the desired text content*

MANIPULATING BULLETS

In the last section, PowerPoint automatically inserted bullets in the Text place-holder when you pressed the **ENTER** key. In this section, you learn how to manip-ulate bullets on a slide to group information. People remember information better when it is "chunked" together, so try to organize your slide text hierarchically. To illustrate the effect of chunking information, consider phone numbers and how much easier they are to remember in the form 708-555-1212 as opposed to 7085551212. You can apply this same principle to your slides using hierarchical bullets.

To promote a point and move it up one level in importance, you indent it to the left using the Promote (Indent Less) button (⬅). To demote a point and move it down one level in importance, you indent it to the right using the Demote (Indent More) button (➡). The Promote (⬅) and Demote (➡) buttons appear on the For-matting toolbar.

Now you practice promoting and demoting bullets.

Perform the following steps . . .

1. Position the insertion point in the text area of "Interactivity."

2. To demote this point:
   CLICK: Demote button (⮕) on the Formatting toolbar
   Notice that the characteristics of the text change. Not only is the text indented but the font size has changed.

3. To return this point to its original position:
   CLICK: Promote (Indent Less) button (⬅)

4. Practice promoting and demoting the two bullets on this slide.

5. Before proceeding to the next section, return both bullets to their original positions.

QUICK REFERENCE
Changing the Indent
Level of Bulleted Items

- CLICK: Promote button (⬅) to indent text to the left
- CLICK: Demote button (⮕) to indent text to the right
- Using the keyboard, press **TAB** to demote text and **SHIFT** + **TAB** to promote text.

ADDING THE REMAINING SLIDES

In this section, you will add the remaining slides to the "Current Trends" presentation.

Perform the following steps . . .

1. To add a third slide to the presentation:
   CHOOSE: New Slide from the Common Tasks toolbar

2. Pick a layout for the new slide from the New Slide dialog box:
   SELECT: Bulleted List
   PRESS: **ENTER** or CLICK: OK

3. CLICK: Title placeholder
   TYPE: **CONNECTIVITY**

4. CLICK: Text placeholder
   TYPE: **Current Trends:**
   PRESS: **ENTER**

5. To type text at a new indent level:
   CLICK: Demote (Indent More) button (⮕)
   TYPE: **Voice mail and e-mail**
   PRESS: **ENTER**
   TYPE: **Telecommuting**
   PRESS: **ENTER**
   TYPE: **Internet-based information**
   Your screen should now appear similar to Figure 2.13.

FIGURE 2.13

SLIDE 3 IN THE
"CURRENT TRENDS"
PRESENTATION

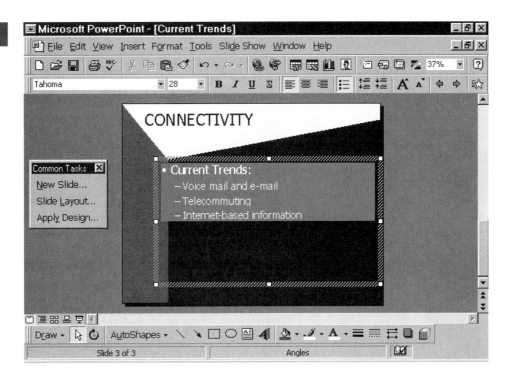

6. To add a fourth slide to the presentation:
   CHOOSE: New Slide from the Common Tasks toolbar

7. Pick a layout for the new slide from the New Slide dialog box:
   SELECT: Bulleted List
   PRESS: (ENTER) or CLICK: OK

8. CLICK: Title placeholder
   TYPE: **INTERACTIVITY**

9. CLICK: Text placeholder
   TYPE: **Current Trends:**
   PRESS: (ENTER)

10. To type text at a new indent level:
    CLICK: Demote (Indent More) button (⇨)
    TYPE: **Multimedia Computers**
    PRESS: (ENTER)
    TYPE: **Personal Digital Assistants**
    PRESS: (ENTER)
    TYPE: **"Internet appliances"**
    Your screen should now appear similar to Figure 2.14.

FIGURE 2.14

SLIDE 4 IN THE "CURRENT
TRENDS" PRESENTATION

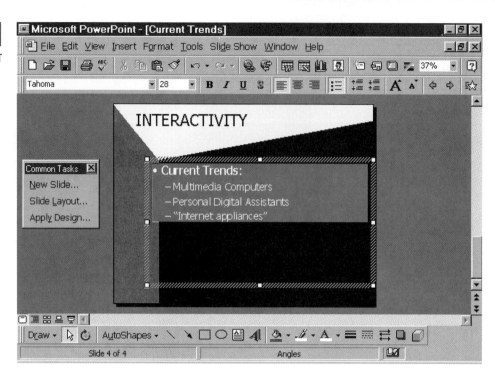

11. To save the presentation:
CLICK: Save button (🖫)

To modify the content of slides you've already created, use the elevator scroll box on the vertical scroll bar (or the double arrows, ⬇ and ⬆, appearing at the bottom of the scroll bar) to move through the presentation. You will practice using the elevator scroll box and arrows later in this session.

Reviewing Your Presentation

To view a presentation as it will appear in its completed form, you use the Slide Show view. To access the Slide Show view, choose View, Slide Show from the Menu bar or click the Slide Show view button (🖵). The presentation fills the entire screen with the current slide, that is, the slide that appears in the presentation window. To view a slide show from the beginning, you must remember to first drag the elevator scroll box to the top of the vertical scroll bar. After you view the last slide in your presentation, the presentation window reappears.

In this section, you view the "Current Trends" presentation.

Perform the following steps . . .

1. DRAG: the elevator scroll box to the top of the vertical scroll bar
Notice that, as you drag the scroll box, the current slide number and first few words of the title appear in the presentation window.

2. CLICK: Slide Show view button (🖵)
The first slide fills the entire screen.

3. To display the next slide:
CLICK: left mouse button

4. To display the previous slide:
PRESS: ⬆

5. Continue by clicking the left mouse button to view the entire presentation. When finished, you are returned to the presentation window where you left off.

Now, let's add some pizzazz to this presentation by inserting some additional graphics to the slides!

EDITING A PRESENTATION

When installing PowerPoint, you have the option of installing the **Clip Gallery,** a collection of images that you can select to include in your presentations. You can also use the Clip Gallery to organize any pictures, sounds, and video clips that you collect. If you choose AutoClipArt from the Tools menu, PowerPoint will analyze the words in your presentation and provide suggestions about which clip art images to use. In this section, you will edit slide 2 of the "Current Trends" presentation to include a picture from the Clip Gallery. You will then resize and move the inserted picture so that it is proportional to the text on the slide. When you are finished, slide 2 will look like Figure 2.15.

FIGURE 2.15

SLIDE 2 WITH THE
INSERTED CLIP ART

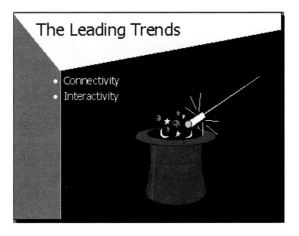

CHANGING THE LAYOUT OF A SLIDE

The easiest way to add clip art or a graphic to an existing slide is to select a new AutoLayout for the slide. First, you make the desired slide active by displaying it in the presentation window. Second, you choose the Slide Layout command from the Common Tasks toolbar. When the Slide Layout dialog box appears, you select a new AutoLayout that includes a clip art or graphic object placeholder and then press **ENTER** or click the Apply command button.

In this section, you practice changing the layout of a slide.

Perform the following steps . . .

1. Ensure that the "Current Trends" presentation appears in the presentation window.

2. To move to slide 2 in the "Current Trends" presentation:
   DRAG: the elevator scroll box downward to display slide 2
   Remember that you can also click the Next Slide (▼) and Previous Slide (▲) buttons on the vertical scroll bar to move through a presentation one slide at a time.

3. To modify the slide's layout to accommodate a clip art image:
   CHOOSE: Slide Layout from the Common Tasks toolbar
   SELECT: Text & Clip Art as the AutoLayout option
   PRESS: (ENTER) or CLICK: Apply
   Your screen should appear similar to Figure 2.16.

FIGURE 2.16

APPLYING THE TEXT & CLIP ART AUTOLAYOUT

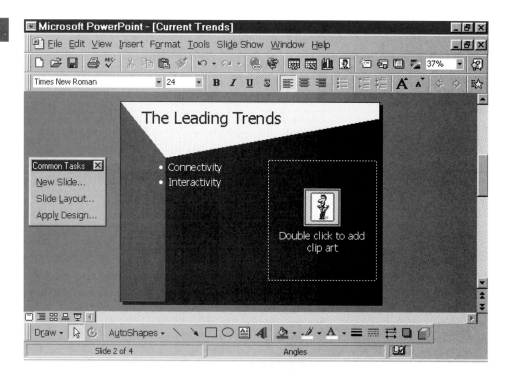

QUICK REFERENCE
Changing the Layout of an Existing Slide

1. Display the slide you want to modify in the presentation window.
2. CHOOSE: Slide Layout from the Common Tasks toolbar
3. SELECT: a new layout in the Slide Layout dialog box
4. PRESS: (ENTER) or CLICK: Apply

INSERTING CLIP ART

In this section, you add a picture from the Clip Gallery to slide 2 of the "Current Trends" presentation. You will then resize and reposition the art to fit nicely on the slide.

Perform the following steps . . .

1. To add clip art to the slide:
DOUBLE-CLICK: clip art placeholder
(*Remember*: You double-click Object placeholders to modify their content.)
The Clip Gallery window appears (Figure 2.17). If this is the first time that you've used the Clip Gallery, it must first gather and categorize the images before you see the dialog box appearing in Figure 2.17. This is a one-time process only. (*Note*: If you do not have the Clip Gallery installed on your computer, contact your instructor or refer to the Microsoft PowerPoint *User's Guide* for further assistance.)

FIGURE 2.17

THE CLIP GALLERY

2. Let's select a picture from the Entertainment category:
SELECT: Entertainment from the list of categories
SELECT: the picture shown in Figure 2.18 from the list of pictures in the dialog box
(*Note*: You may have to drag the scroll box downward to see this picture.)

3. To add the picture to your slide:
PRESS: (**ENTER**) or CLICK: Insert
Your screen should now appear similar to Figure 2.18. The clip art image is inserted and is currently selected. You know the object is selected because it is surrounded by selection handles, which look like small boxes. Notice also that the Picture toolbar now appears on your screen. You can use this toolbar to perform tasks such as changing the shape and color of the selected image. The Picture toolbar only appears when you select a picture object.

FIGURE 2.18

ADDING A CLIP ART IMAGE TO THE "CURRENT TRENDS" PRESENTATION

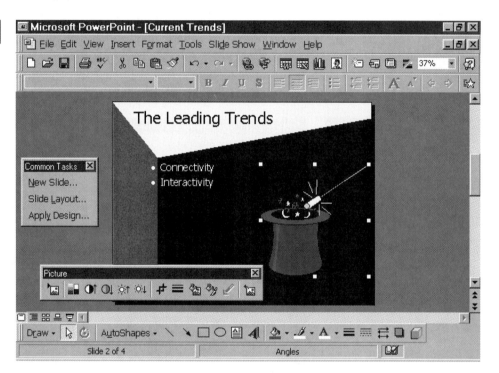

4. To resize a picture, you select it by clicking once on the object and then dragging its selection handles inward or outward. You use the corner handles to size an object larger or smaller, while maintaining its relative proportions. To move the picture, you position the mouse pointer in the center of the object and drag the object to another location on the slide.

5. Practice sizing and moving the picture to make it appear as similar to Figure 2.15 as possible.

6. To save your editing changes:
CLICK: Save button (🖫)

QUICK REFERENCE Inserting Clip Art	1. **In the presentation window, display the slide you want to modify.** 2. **CHOOSE: Slide Layout from the Common Tasks toolbar** 3. **SELECT: an AutoLayout option with a clip art placeholder** 4. **PRESS:** ENTER **or CLICK: Apply** 5. **DOUBLE-CLICK: clip art placeholder** 6. **SELECT: a clip art image from the Clip Gallery** 7. **PRESS:** ENTER **or CLICK: OK**

QUICK REFERENCE Resizing and Moving Clip Art	1. **SELECT: clip art object by clicking the mouse pointer once over the object (handles appear around the picture when properly selected)** 2. **DRAG: a handle on the object to size the picture, or** **DRAG: the center of the object to move the picture**

USING THE STYLE CHECKER

Before you print a presentation, review it using PowerPoint's **Style Checker.** The Style Checker studies your presentation for spelling errors, visual clarity, and the proper use of punctuation. You respond to the Style Checker's suggestions by clicking the Change or Ignore buttons. Figure 2.19 shows the Style Checker dialog box. The Options command button enables you to further customize what the Style Checker checks for in order to match your company's particular style. For example, let's say that you always want your presentations to use a 32-point size for the text on a Title slide, no more than two fonts or five bullets on any given slide, and all bulleted text to end without a period. You can establish each of these style rules, as well as many others, using the Options button.

FIGURE 2.19

THE STYLE CHECKER
DIALOG BOX

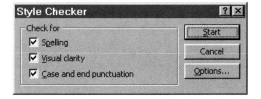

In this section, you use the Style Checker to review the "Current Trends" presentation.

Perform the following steps . . .

1. Ensure that slide 1 of the "Current Trends" presentation appears in the presentation window.

2. To activate the Style Checker:
   CHOOSE: Tools, Style Checker

3. Before starting the Style Checker, let's look at some of the options that are available to you. Do the following:
   CLICK: Options command button
   CLICK: *Case and End Punctuation* tab and review the options
   CLICK: *Visual Clarity* tab and review the options
   Figure 2.20 shows the contents of the two tabs.

FIGURE 2.20

THE STYLE CHECKER
DIALOG BOX: OPTIONS

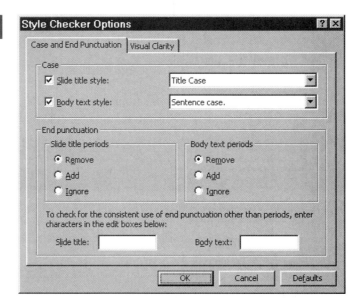

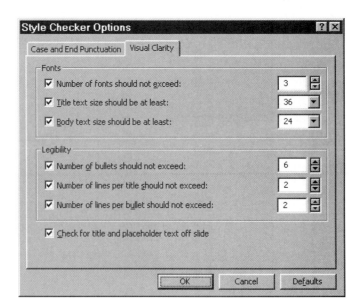

4. To return to the Style Checker dialog box and start the process:
CLICK: Cancel button
CLICK: Start button

5. Proceed by clicking the Ignore button if the Style Checker finds any spelling suggestions and style inconsistency remarks.

QUICK REFERENCE
Using the Style Checker

1. **CHOOSE: Tools, Style Checker**
2. **Use the Options button to customize style settings, as desired.**
3. **Respond to the Style Checker's suggestions by clicking the Ignore or Change buttons.**

PRINTING A PRESENTATION

Now that you've created a presentation, this section explains how to send it to the printer. This section provides only a brief glimpse at the tools available.

The quickest method for sending a presentation to the printer is to click the Print button (🖨) on the Standard toolbar. When you click this button, no dialog boxes appear asking you to confirm your choice, so ensure that the printer is online and has sufficient paper. You can also use the File, Print command to print a document, which causes the Print dialog box to display (Figure 2.21). After making selections, you press **ENTER** or click OK to proceed.

FIGURE 2.21

PRINT DIALOG BOX

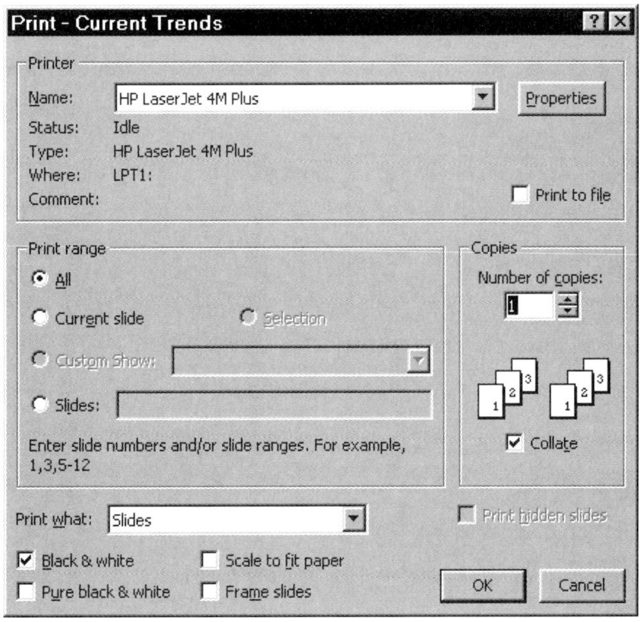

Now you will print a presentation.

Perform the following steps . . .

1. To print the "Current Trends" presentation:
   CHOOSE: File, Print
   The Print dialog box appears. (*Note*: You can also press the `CTRL`+p shortcut key to display the Print dialog box.)

2. At this point, PowerPoint assumes that you want to print the slides in the current presentation window. To see the other options:
   CLICK: down arrow beside the *Print what* drop-down list box

3. To print all of the slides in the presentation:
   SELECT: Slides (the default selection)
   PRESS: `ENTER` or CLICK: OK

4. Close the presentation window and exit PowerPoint. (*Note*: Do not save the changes to the presentation file.)

QUICK REFERENCE
Printing a Presentation

1. **CHOOSE: File, Print from the menu**
2. **SELECT: what you want to print in the *Print what* drop-down list box**
3. **PRESS: `ENTER` or CLICK: OK**

Summary

This session introduced you to the fundamentals of creating a presentation. You used one of PowerPoint's intelligent helpers, the AutoContent Wizard, to assist you in structuring and designing your presentation. You then created another presentation by picking a design template and added slides to the presentation by choosing New Slide from the Common Tasks toolbar. This session also introduced you to saving, viewing, and editing a slide presentation. You manipulated the text and bullets on a slide in addition to changing its layout and adding clip art. Finally, you performed a style check on a presentation and learned how to print a slide presentation.

COMMAND SUMMARY

Many of the commands and procedures appearing in this session are provided in Table 2.1.

TABLE 2.1

Command Summary

Task Description	Menu Command	Alternative Method
Create a new presentation	File, New	
Save a presentation to the disk	File, Save	
Save a presentation to a new location or to a different name	File, Save As	
Select all the text in a placeholder	Edit, Select All	(ENTER)+a
Change the layout of a slide	Format, Slide Layout	Choose Slide Layout from the Common Tasks toolbar
Use the Style Checker	Tools, Style Checker	
Print a presentation	File, Print	

KEY TERMS

AutoContent Wizard

A PowerPoint tool that leads you through creating the structure for your presentation.

AutoLayout

In PowerPoint, a slide format with text and graphic placeholders. You select an AutoLayout for a head start when adding a new slide to a presentation.

build slides

In PowerPoint, a slide in which the bullet points are displayed one at a time.

Clip Gallery

A collection of professionally designed images that you can include in your presentations.

default presentation format

The design template that is in effect when you start by choosing the Blank Presentation option.

design template

A design template is a presentation whose background, color scheme, typefaces, and other formatting options can be applied to another presentation.

masters

The slide, outline, and notes page templates that determine how the standard slides, outlines, and notes pages are formatted and will appear in a presentation. Any visuals that you include on a master will print on every page in the presentation.

object

In PowerPoint, an object is an individual element on a slide. It can be text, a graphic, a picture, a shape, a video clip, and so on.

placeholders

In PowerPoint, slide locations where you enter titles, sub-titles, main text, clip art, graphs, and organizational charts.

presentation template

A presentation template is a presentation whose subject outline can be applied to another presentation.

Style Checker

Using this PowerPoint tool, you can review your presentation for spelling errors, clarity of visual style, and use of punctuation.

transition

In PowerPoint, an effect used in computer-based presentations to dissolve or wipe one slide from the screen before the next appears.

EXERCISES

SHORT ANSWER

1. What are the basic steps for creating a presentation?

2. What elements of your presentation does the AutoContent Wizard help you define?

3. Provide some specific examples of how you might customize the Style Checker to your needs.

4. How do you insert a new slide in a presentation?

5. How would you go about changing the font size of the text in a text box all at once?

6. What is the procedure for printing a presentation using the menu?

7. How do you change a slide's AutoLayout?

8. How do you manipulate bullet levels on a slide?

9. What is the procedure for resizing a clip art image?

10. When would you want to use the File, Save As command rather than the File, Save command?

HANDS-ON

(*Note*: Ensure that you know the location of your Advantage Files and where to store your Data Files. If necessary, ask your instructor or lab assistant for additional information.)

1. Perform the following steps to create a three-slide presentation named "Using Color." The objective of your presentation is to describe some guidelines for using color in on-screen presentations.

   a. Load Microsoft PowerPoint.

   b. Create a new on-screen presentation using a design template.
      CHOOSE: File, New
      CLICK: *Presentation Designs* tab

   c. Select the Contemporary Portrait template design.

   d. Select the Title Slide AutoLayout from the New Slide dialog box.

   e. The title of your presentation is:
      Using Color Wisely

   f. The sub-title of your presentation is:
      By
      your name

   g. Add a second slide to the presentation, based on the Bulleted List layout, with the following information.

      Title:
      Keep it Simple
      Bullet 1: **Choose colors properly to make powerful statements**
      Bullet 2: **Too many colors or unnecessary colors can dilute the effect**

   h. Add a third slide to the presentation, based on the Bulleted List layout, with the following information.

      Title:
      Target Your Output Needs
      Bullet 1: **For 35 mm slides, pick dark backgrounds**
      Bullet 2: **For overhead transparencies, pick light backgrounds**

   i. Display the presentation using Slide Show view.

   j. Return to the Slide view.

   k. Save the presentation as "Using Color" to your Data Files location.

2. In this exercise, you edit slide 3 of the "Using Color" presentation that you created in the last exercise to look like Figure 2.22. Make sure to do the following:

    a. Change the layout of slide 3 to the Text & Clip Art layout.

    b. Add the picture of a target to the slide. (*Hint*: The target is located in the Sports & Leisure category of the Microsoft Clip Gallery).

    c. In Slide view, resize the clip art image so it appears similar to Figure 2.22.

FIGURE 2.22

SLIDE 3 OF THE "USING COLOR" PRESENTATION

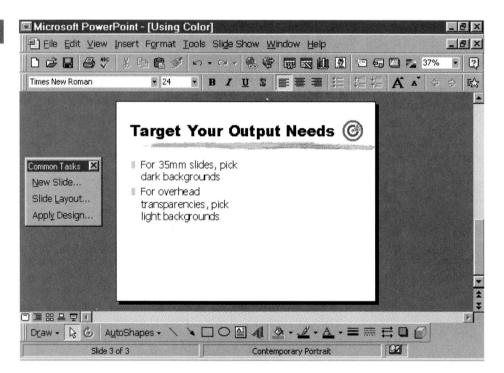

    d. Display the presentation using Slide Show view.

    e. Return to Slide view.

    f. Print the entire presentation.

    g. Save the "Using Color" presentation back to your Data Files location.

    h. Close the presentation.

3. Create a presentation for the five slides shown in Figure 2.23. Save the presentation to your Data Files location as "Advertising."

FIGURE 2.23

SLIDE 1

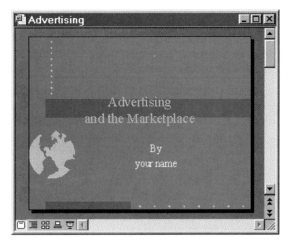

SLIDE 2

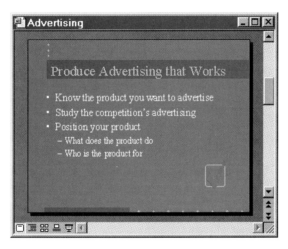

SLIDE 3

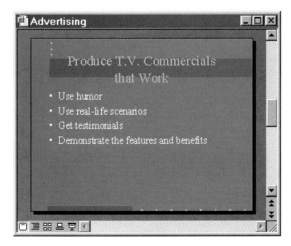

SLIDE 4

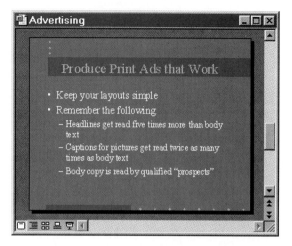

SLIDE 5

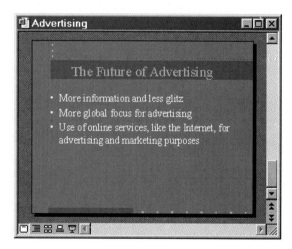

4. In this exercise, you create a presentation that contains the information shown below. On your own, decide which design template and layouts to use to best present the information. When you are finished, save the presentation as "Storage" to your Data Files location.

    Harold Harvey's Self-Storage
    You can't beat our prices!
    1- 800-HAR-VEYS

    Full range of sizes and features:
    Choose from small, medium, and large storage units. We will even customize the interior of your unit to meet your unique requirements.

    Climate controlled:
    Worried about weather extremes? Don't bother! All storage units are climate controlled.

Protected environment

- *All of our locations are fenced and lighted, and use 24-hour video surveillance.*

- *A resident manager is present at each location. If you have questions or concerns, just pick up the phone.*

Rental trucks available free:
If you're just moving in to Harold Harvey's Self-Storage, we'll provide you with a rental truck—FREE.

CALL US!
Your name
Sales representative

5. On your own, create the contents of your own personal web site using PowerPoint's "Personal Home Page (Online)" presentation template. Begin by choosing File, New from the Menu bar. Then select the "Personal Home Page (Online)" template from the *Presentations* tab. Proceed by filling in the information requested on each slide. When you're finished, save the presentation as "On Your Own-1" to your Data Files location.

6. On your own, create a presentation on a topic you're interested in (e.g., hiking, traveling, or reading.) Include between five and eight slides and at least one clip art picture. Save the presentation as "On Your Own-2" to your Data Files location.

(*Note*: In the following case problems, assume the role of the primary characters and perform the same steps that they identify. You may want to re-read the session opening.)

1. Sharon Rheingold is on a mission. After several evenings of study at the campus computer lab, she is now comfortable using Microsoft PowerPoint to create simple presentations. Fortunately, her roommate Walt had time to show her the AutoContent Wizard and how to use design templates. With the start of classes only a few days away, Sharon is ready to put her first lecture together using PowerPoint.

    Her schedule being quite tight this past week, Sharon was only able to jot down rough notes for her outline:

    Course Title: Public Speaking 101
    Instructor: Sharon Rheingold

    Lecture 1: An Introduction to Public Speaking

    Five Cs for Excellence in Public Speaking
    - *Confident*
    - *Competent*
    - *Credible*
    - *Convincing*
    - *Comfortable*

    Reasons for Experiencing Stage Fright
    - *Fear of failure*
    - *Lack of confidence*
    - *Lack of preparation*
    - *Lack of knowledge about topic*
    - *Lack of knowledge about audience*

    Methods for Overcoming Stage Fright
    - *Be positive*
    - *Practice often*
    - *Prepare thoroughly*
    - *Research your topic*
    - *Research your audience*

    Now Sharon has to enter these notes into PowerPoint in order to create color overhead transparencies. Since her content is fairly well organized, she decides to use one of PowerPoint's presentation design templates. In addition to an opening slide introducing the course and herself, Sharon calculates that the presentation only requires one outline slide for the lecture and three content slides for each of her main discussion topics. At the last minute, she decides to add a closing slide that thanks the students for attending the presentation and wishes them luck for the coming semester. Sharon saves the presentation as "Public Speaking 101" to her Data Files location and prints the six slides for review.

2. An experienced public speaker herself, Sharon knows the importance of practicing her presentation before she has to deliver it in front of an audience. She uses PowerPoint's Slide Show view to go through the "Public Speaking 101" presentation and then reviews it again in the Slide Sorter view. "Almost there!" she thinks to herself.

Although she feels comfortable with the presentation, Sharon notices that the lecture may be too short. After not much deliberation, Sharon decides to add one more slide to the presentation. Using Slide view, she displays the last content slide titled "Methods for Overcoming Stage Fright" and then clicks the New Slide button on the Status bar. She adds a slide with the following content and then revises her outline slide at the beginning of the presentation.

Types of Presentations
- *Technical (for technical specifications)*
- *Instructional (for communicating a process)*
- *Illustrative (with anecdotal stories)*
- *Demonstrative (with live demonstration)*
- *Discussion (for informal group meetings)*

Again, Sharon practices the presentation using the Slide view and then saves it and prints it out on the laser printer for Walt to review.

3. Walt returned late from his part-time job after three hours of overtime and was not in the best of moods to review Sharon's presentation. "Why is there so much text here?" exclaimed Walt, rubbing his eyes and trying to focus on the pages Sharon had handed to him. "Can't you put a couple of pictures in this thing to liven it up a little?" Walt walked slowly across the living room and then looked up, "You should have used the Clip Gallery to add some pictures. I know there's one picture in there of a person standing at a podium. You can use that one for this "Five Cs" slide. And for the last slide, don't just say "Thank You". Insert a fun graphic to let them know that they're in the best public speaking section on campus!"

Sharon thought about Walt's comments and took each to heart. She would add some pictures to her presentation using the Clip Gallery, perform one more practice run, and then print out the final presentation for her students.

Save Sharon's presentation as "Public Speaking 101" to the Data Files location.

4. During morning coffee, Dr. Tomas Ritchie, the law faculty's premier authority on Canadian business law, listened intently to Dr. Antoski's enthusiastic recount of Sharon Rheingold's first class. Since Tomas had known Sharon for two years, he was not surprised with Kirsten's glowing report of his star pupil. However, he was quite surprised that Sharon was a skilled computer user and could prepare such high-quality materials. He would definitely keep this fact in mind for future projects!

Two weeks later, Dr. Ritchie approached Sharon to ask her help in preparing a lecture he was conducting for the American Business Association. The presentation, "Understanding Canadian Business Law," was to be delivered the next day at the association's annual general meeting. The original speaker had canceled at the last moment, due to a family emergency, and Dr. Ritchie was contacted as her replacement. Fortunately, the original speaker had already arranged the equipment and room for a computer-based presentation. The only item Dr. Ritchie was missing was the presentation!

Dr. Ritchie showed Sharon a quick outline and asked her to prepare a "computerized slide show." He didn't have any details for content and would most likely have to "wing it" at the podium. However, he wanted her to produce an introductory slide with his name and the name of the presentation, along with a separate slide for each topic he was going to discuss. The topics included:

The Law of Torts in Canada
- *The tort concept*
- *Elements of a tort*
- *Burden of proof*
- *Professional liability*

Types of Contracts
- *Contract of sale*
- *Contract of employment*

Formation of a Contract
- *Offer and acceptance*
- *Consideration*
- *Intention to enter into a contract*
- *Capacity to contract*
- *Requirement of writing*

Effects of and Remedies for a Breach of Contract
- *What is a breach?*
- *Express repudiation*
- *Damages*
- *Quantum meruit*

Forms of Business Organization
- *Sole proprietorship*
- *Partnership*
- *Corporation*

Knowing that Dr. Ritchie would be a great ally in coming years, Sharon wanted to do everything she could to impress her advisor. She created and printed the presentation in less than an hour, handing it to him just as he was about to leave for home. Sharon would have to remember to thank Walt for introducing her to Microsoft PowerPoint!

Save this presentation as "Canadian Law" to your Data Files location.

Microsoft PowerPoint 97 for Windows

Designing a Presentation

SESSION OUTLINE

Applying Templates

Editing Masters

The Importance of Color

Viewing Slides in Black and White

Working More with Text

Working with AutoShapes

Summary

Key Terms

Exercises

INTRODUCTION

In this session, you learn to use some of Power-Point's more productive features, including methods that help you take control of your presentations. You soon discover that when it comes to designing a presentation in PowerPoint, you have endless options at your fingertips. Rather than show you every design and productivity feature, this session concentrates on the most commonly used tools.

CASE STUDY	**H2 UNDERSCAPING LTD.**

In 1989 Chip Yee started H2 UnderScaping Ltd. (H2U), a landscaping operation that sells and installs underground sprinkler systems. Since that time, H2U has grown from annual sales of $30,000 to its current year's projection of over $700,000. Now that his employees perform most of the administrative duties and manual labor, Chip has more time on his hands to get involved in the community.

Chip is an active member in both the local Chamber of Commerce and the Downtown Business Association. The Chamber's president, Mrs. Vi Krieg, recently approached Chip to ask him to act as spokesperson at this year's Business Show. Specifically, Vi asked Chip to prepare an electronic presentation for the evening banquet and emphasized that there would be representatives from neighboring Chambers in the audience. Obviously the president wants to impress her peers with their group's professionalism and technical proficiency!

Fortunately, Chip is familiar with Microsoft Office and has become quite good at using Microsoft Word. Although he has created only one or two simple presentations in PowerPoint, Chip has discovered that the programs in Microsoft Office work alike in many ways, making them easy to learn and use. But this presentation would be challenging. In addition to creating a content-rich presentation, Chip will have to pull off an Oscar-winning performance to satisfy Mrs. Krieg.

In this session, you and Chip learn about some features for making your PowerPoint presentations stand out from the crowd. Rather than relying on PowerPoint's stock designs, you learn to enhance the design templates, edit the Slide Master, and utilize color. In addition, you customize bullets, manipulate text in Outline view, and learn to position text anywhere on a slide. Good luck to you both!

APPLYING TEMPLATES

Using templates is like having the fastest graphics design specialist as part of your staff. Fortunately for you, PowerPoint's graphics design specialist knows over 100 different designs and lets you apply any one of them to your presentations. Just think of the time savings—after typing the content for a presentation in Outline view, you simply pick and choose from multiple design templates to finalize the look and feel of your presentation for a particular audience. You could even deliver the same presentation to two different groups using two different design templates.

If you can remember back to Session 2, you chose a design template named "angles." This template uses red, black, and white to divide the slide into three visual areas. All of PowerPoint's templates, including the "angles" template, are stored in separate files on the hard disk. Actually, a template is defined as any presentation whose design and format specifications you want to apply to another presentation.

Not only can you pick from the templates provided by PowerPoint, any presentation you create can serve as a template for another presentation. The advantage of using PowerPoint's templates is that they were all created by professional artists and presentation designers. To apply a template, choose Format, Apply Design from the menu or choose Apply Design from the Common Tasks toolbar. In the Apply Design dialog box that appears, you select the desired template and then click the Apply command button.

In this section, you apply a different template to a presentation.

Perform the following steps . . .

1. Make sure that you have identified the location for retrieving your Advantage Files and for saving your Data Files. If you require a diskette, place it in the diskette drive now.

2. Open the "Chili" presentation from the Advantage Files location. The first slide of the "Chili" presentation should appear in the presentation window (Figure 3.1).

FIGURE 3.1

"CHILI" PRESENTATION

3. Review the contents of this presentation. Do the following:
   CLICK: Slide Show view button
   CLICK: left mouse button repeatedly, until you've run through the entire presentation
   When you have viewed all the slides, PowerPoint will display the first slide of your presentation in Slide view.

4. To select a new template for the presentation:
   CHOOSE: Apply Design from the Common Tasks toolbar
   (*Note:* If the Common Tasks toolbar doesn't appear, right-click one of the currently displayed toolbars and then choose Common Tasks from the toolbar menu.) The Apply Design dialog box appears, as shown in Figure 3.2.

FIGURE 3.2

APPLY DESIGN TEMPLATE
DIALOG BOX

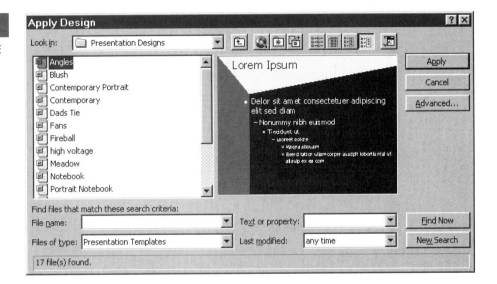

5. The templates are listed in alphabetical order. Using the mouse, click on several templates in the template list box. You will notice that a representation of the selected template appears in the area to the right. Before proceeding to the next step:
   SELECT: "Dads Tie" from the list of templates
   PRESS: ENTER or CLICK: Apply
   The new template will be applied to every slide in your presentation. When finished, your screen should appear similar to Figure 3.3.

FIGURE 3.3

THE "CHILI"
PRESENTATION USING
THE DAD'S TIE DESIGN
TEMPLATE

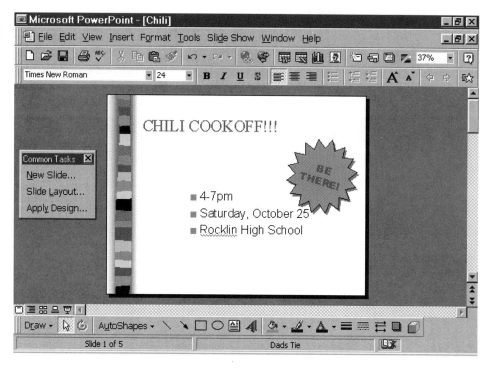

6. To get a better feel for how the template actually looks:
    CLICK: Slide Show view button (⬛)
    CLICK: left mouse button repeatedly, until you've run through the entire
    presentation

7. After being returned from Slide Show view to Slide view in the presentation
    window, save the presentation as "Chili Cookoff" with the new template:
    CHOOSE: File, Save As
    TYPE: Chili Cookoff in the *File name* text box
    CLICK: down arrow beside the Look in drop-down list box
    SELECT: *your Data Files location*
    PRESS: (ENTER) or CLICK: Save command button

QUICK REFERENCE
Applying a New Template
to an Existing Presentation

1. **Open the desired presentation and switch to Slide view.**

2. **CHOOSE: Apply Design from the Common Tasks toolbar, or**
    CHOOSE: Format, Apply Design from the Menu bar

3. **SELECT: a template from the Apply Design dialog box**

4. **PRESS: (ENTER) or CLICK: Apply**

IN ADDITION DOWNLOADING ADDITIONAL TEMPLATES FROM THE WEB

If you have access to the World Wide Web, you can download additional templates and wizards from Microsoft's Web site. To do this:

1. CHOOSE: Help, Microsoft on the Web

2. CHOOSE: Free Stuff

Then follow the instructions on the Web page to download the files you want.

EDITING MASTERS

PowerPoint provides a master page for each element of your presentation: slides, handouts, and notes pages. Any text, graphic, or other object that you place on a master page appears on every page of that type in the presentation. For example, you can place your company's logo on the Handout Master so that it prints out on every handout page automatically. PowerPoint lets you edit the following types of masters:

- *Slide Master*   The Slide Master holds the formatting for all the titles, main text, and background placeholders in your presentation. To edit the Slide Master, hold down **SHIFT** and click the Slide view button (▢). Or choose View, Master, Slide Master from the Menu bar.

- *Title Master*   The Title Master holds the formatting for any slides in your presentation that use the Title Slide layout. Unless you edit the Title Master, title slides conform to the Slide Master. To edit the Title Master, choose View, Master, Title Master from the Menu bar.

- *Handout Master*   The Handout Master holds the formatting for the appearance of headers and footers on handout pages. To edit the Handout Master, hold down **SHIFT** and click the Outline View button (▤) or the Slide Sorter View button (▦). Or choose View, Master, Handout Master from the Menu bar.

- *Notes Master*   The Notes Master holds the formatting for your Notes pages. To edit the Notes Master, hold down **SHIFT** and click the Notes Page view button (▣). Or choose View, Master, Notes Master from the Menu bar.

In this section, you edit the Slide Master for the "Chili Cookoff" presentation. The slides in this presentation use two different design layouts. Slides 2, 3, and 5 use the *Title Slide* layout and slides 1 and 4 use the *Bulleted List* layout. If you were to edit the Title Master, only slides 2, 3, and 5 would be affected. However, in the following section, you edit the Slide Master which will affect all slides in the presentation.

EDITING THE SLIDE MASTER

To help you imagine the contents of an actual slide, PowerPoint inserts Title and Text placeholders on the Title and Slide Masters. However, you do not type text into the placeholders—they are there only to show you the formatting specifications. If you want text to appear on every slide in your presentation, you must use the Drawing toolbar, described later in this session.

You will now change the appearance of all the titles in your presentation by editing the Slide Master.

Perform the following steps . . .

1. Assuming that you just completed the last section, slide 1 of the "Chili Cookoff" presentation should appear in the presentation window. If it doesn't appear, retrieve it from your Data Files location. Ensure that you are viewing slide 1 in Slide view before proceeding.

2. To practice changing the Slide Master:
CHOOSE: View, Master, Slide Master
Your screen should now appear similar to Figure 3.4.

FIGURE 3.4

THE SLIDE MASTER FOR THE "CHILI COOKOFF" PRESENTATION

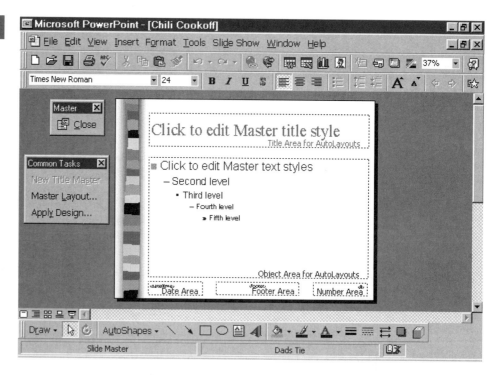

3. Currently, the titles of the slides in this presentation are displayed using Times New Roman. To include italic formatting in the title:
CLICK: Master title placeholder (which appears as "Click to edit Master title style")
CLICK: Italic button (*I*) on the Formatting toolbar
Notice that you do not need to select the text in the placeholder to change its formatting characteristics. You simply position the insertion point in the placeholder.

4. To preview the slides using the new format:
    CLICK: Slide view button ([⬛])
    Notice that the title of slide 1 is italicized.

5. To view the next slide:
    CLICK: Next Slide button ([⬇]) on the vertical scroll bar
    Notice that the title of slide 2 is also italicized.

6. View the remaining slides in the presentation and notice that all the main
    titles are italicized.

In this and subsequent sessions, as you learn more about designing a presentation
and adding visuals, you will periodically make changes to the Slide Master. In general, however, you should edit the Slide Master only when you want to change the
format of the entire presentation.

QUICK REFERENCE	1. **Open the desired presentation and switch to Slide view.**
Editing the Title and Slide Masters	2. **CHOOSE: View, Master, Title Master to edit all Title slides**
	CHOOSE: View, Master, Slide Master to edit all other slides
	3. **Edit the Title and Text placeholders on the Title and Slide Masters, add text boxes, insert graphics and charts, and add other objects as desired.**
	4. **CHOOSE: View, Slides to return to Slide view**

EDITING AN INDIVIDUAL SLIDE

As you learned in the last section, if you want to format more than one slide at
once, change the Title or Slide Master. Otherwise, modify individual slides. It is
important to note that any changes you make to individual slides are considered
exceptions to the Slide Master. If you later change the Slide Master or apply a
design template, PowerPoint applies the new format but retains your exceptions.
In this section, you learn to edit an individual slide in the "Chili Cookoff" presentation.

You will now remove the italic attribute from the first slide of the "Chili Cookoff"
presentation and add the bold attribute.

Perform the following steps . . .

1. Ensure that you are viewing slide 2 in Slide view before proceeding.

2. Unlike formatting the Master title placeholder in the last section, formatting
    a single title requires that you first select all the text in the Title place-
    holder. To do so:
    CLICK: in the Title placeholder
    CHOOSE: Edit, Select All
    (*Hint:* You can also drag the I-beam mouse pointer across the text or press
    [CTRL]+a to quickly select all the text in a placeholder.)

3. To remove the italic attribute and apply boldface to the selection:
CLICK: Italic button (I) to turn off the italic attribute
CLICK: Bold button (B) to turn on the bold attribute

4. To remove the active selection from the placeholder:
CLICK: anywhere outside the placeholder area (e.g., click near the top right-hand corner of the slide)
Slide 2 should now look similar to Figure 3.5. Slide 2 no longer conforms to the Slide Master. If you make a formatting change in the Slide Master, for example, all the slides in your presentation will change *except* for slide 2.

FIGURE 3.5

SLIDE 2 AFTER
FORMATTING THE TITLE

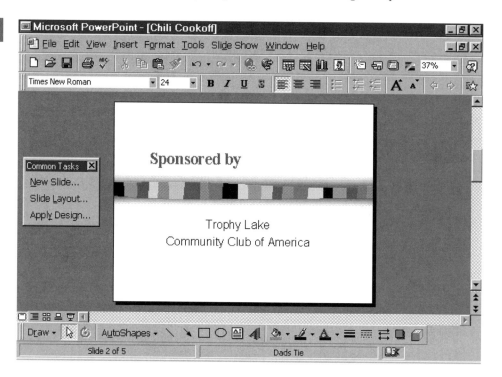

5. But what if you want slide 2 to reinherit the Slide Master attributes so that it will change along with the other slides? To do so, perform the following:
CHOOSE: Slide Layout from the Common Tasks toolbar
CLICK: Reapply button
The text now conforms to the Slide Master once again.

QUICK REFERENCE
Reapplying the Slide Master
Format to a Slide

1. **Make the desired slide active in the presentation window.**

2. **CHOOSE: Slide Layout from the Common Tasks toolbar, or**
   CHOOSE: Format, Slide Layout

3. **CLICK: Reapply command button**

THE IMPORTANCE OF COLOR

The colors used in a presentation can influence how an audience responds to your message. Colors not only bring emotion to a presentation, they communicate its formality. For example, a presentation that uses deep blues and grays better suits IBM's serious image than Apple's flamboyant image. Used improperly, colors can also undermine your presentation's theme and distract the audience. You would not want to use red, the internationally recognized color for "stop," as the background color for a presentation on entrepreneurship. You should also be aware that a significant portion of your audience—especially adult males—may be colorblind and not perceive the differences between two or more colors. Keeping all these points in mind, you are best advised to keep your color selection simple and restrained.

Fortunately for us, Microsoft hired professional artists to compile PowerPoint's numerous color schemes. A **color scheme** is a set of eight colors that you can apply to individual slides, notes pages, and audience handouts. The eight main colors include a background color, text and line color, shadows color, title text color, fill color, and three colors for accents. By using color schemes, you ensure that all the colors in your presentation are balanced and will work well together. Also, color schemes make it easy to apply a new set of colors to your presentation, just as using templates makes it easy to change its overall design.

To experiment with the colors that are available, you can choose Format, Slide Color Scheme from the menu to display the Color Scheme dialog box (shown in Figure 3.6). Using the *Standard* tab, you can choose one of six preset color schemes that change the way colors are used for all the objects on your slides. These schemes include a mixture of light and dark backgrounds and colors for the slide objects. As a general rule of thumb, you should pick darker backgrounds for 35 mm slides and on-screen presentations, and light background colors for overhead transparencies.

The *Custom* tab gives you control over individual slide objects. When you are satisfied with your color selections, you select the Apply command button to apply the new color scheme to the current slide or the Apply to All command button to change the entire presentation. It is important to note that the Apply to All option changes the color scheme for the Slide Master as well.

FIGURE 3.6

COLOR SCHEME DIALOG
BOX: STANDARD TAB

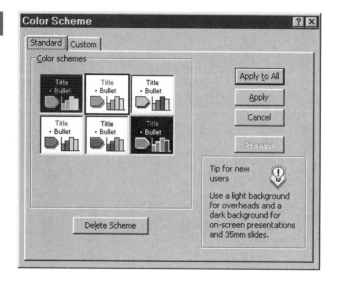

EDITING THE CURRENT COLOR SCHEME

In this section, you change the colors used in the "Chili Cookoff" presentation.

 **Perform the following steps . . .**

1. Ensure that you are viewing slide 1 in Slide view before proceeding.

2. CHOOSE: Format, Slide Color Scheme
   The dialog box in Figure 3.6 should appear. The scheme shown in the center of the top row is currently applied to your presentation.

3. Experiment with how your slides would look with a few of the other schemes by doing the following:
   SELECT: a color scheme
   CLICK: Preview button
   DRAG: Color Scheme dialog box to reveal more of the preview image

4. DRAG: Color Scheme dialog box back to its original position

5. Repeat steps 3 and 4 to view a few more color schemes.

6. To pick the original color scheme:
   SELECT: the color scheme in the center of the first row
   You may find that a standard color scheme works well for you. If not, you will want to create a color scheme that is customized to your needs.

7. To change the color for individual slide objects, do the following:
   CLICK: *Custom* tab
   The Color Scheme dialog box should appear similar to Figure 3.7.

FIGURE 3.7

COLOR SCHEME DIALOG
BOX: CUSTOM TAB

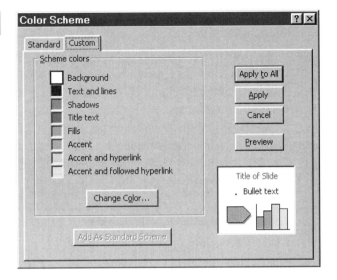

FIGURE 3.7

COLOR SCHEME DIALOG
BOX: CUSTOM TAB

8. To modify the foreground or text color for the Title placeholder:
CLICK: *Title Text* color box (in the *Scheme Colors* area)
CLICK: Change Color command button
The Title Text Color dialog box appears (Figure 3.8). The default color
palette appears. You select different colors by pointing to them in the
palette and then clicking. (*Note:* You can mix your own colors using the
Custom tab.)

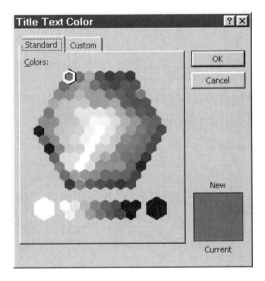

FIGURE 3.8

TITLE TEXT COLOR
DIALOG BOX

9. Black is the currently selected color for title text.
SELECT: a different color in the color palette
CLICK: OK command button

10. To apply the new color to the current slide only:
CLICK: Apply command button
Notice that the new color has been incorporated into the current slide.

11. On your own, display the other slides in the "Chili Cookoff" presentation. You'll notice that they still conform to the Slide Master's color scheme. When you are done, return to viewing slide 1 in Slide view.

12. To reapply the original color scheme to slide 1:
CHOOSE: Format, Slide Color Scheme
CLICK: *Standard* tab
SELECT: the original color scheme (top row, center)
CLICK: Apply command button
Slide 1 should now conform to the original color scheme.

QUICK REFERENCE Changing an Individual Color	1. **CHOOSE: Format, Slide Color Scheme** 2. **CLICK: *Custom* tab** 3. **SELECT: a slide object (in the Scheme Colors area)** 4. **CLICK: Change Color command button** 5. **SELECT: a new color in the color palette** 6. **CLICK: Apply to change the color on the current slide, or** **CLICK: Apply to All to change the color for all slides**

QUICK REFERENCE Reapply the Slide Master Colors	1. **Make the desired slide active in the presentation window.** 2. **CHOOSE: Format, Slide Color Scheme** 3. **CLICK: *Standard* tab** 4. **SELECT: the master color scheme (in the Color Schemes area)** 5. **CLICK: Apply command button**

VIEWING SLIDES IN BLACK AND WHITE

Depending on how you plan to output your presentation, you may at some point want to see how your presentation looks in black and white. This feature is especially relevant if you plan to print slides, handouts, or notes pages on a black and white laser printer. To view your presentation in black and white, click the Black and White view button (🖼) on the Standard toolbar or choose View, Black and White from the Menu bar. PowerPoint will automatically convert your on-screen colors to black, white, and shades of gray. In this view mode, you can also change how selected objects appear by choosing Black and White from the shortcut menu and then choosing a display option.

In the following steps, you view the "Chili Cookoff" presentation in Black and White View.

Perform the following steps . . .

1. Ensure that you are viewing slide 3 of the "Chili Cookoff" presentation before continuing.

2. To display the presentation in black and white:
CLICK: Black and White view button ()
The slide has been converted to shades of black and white. Notice that PowerPoint also displays a color miniature of the current slide.

3. Point to the Title placeholder in the top of the window and then right-click to display the shortcut menu.

4. CHOOSE: Black and White
Your screen should appear similar to Figure 3.9. Using the options on the shortcut menu, you can change the appearance of the selected object or choose "Don't Show" to remove the object from view.

FIGURE 3.9

BLACK AND WHITE
SHORTCUT MENU

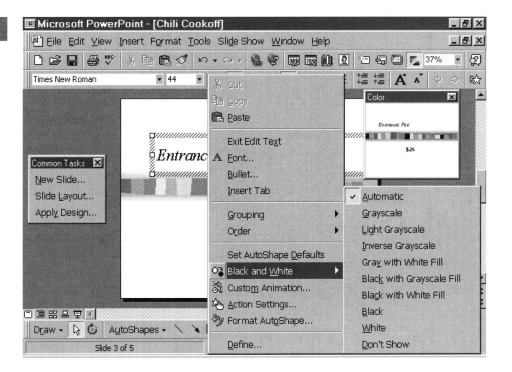

5. To remove the shortcut menu, click anywhere in the presentation window.

6. To switch back to color mode:
CLICK: Black and White view button ()

QUICK REFERENCE
Viewing a Presentation in Black and White

1. CLICK: Black and White view button (), or
CHOOSE: View, Black and White

2. Change the way objects appear by choosing Black and White from the shortcut menu and then choosing an available option.

WORKING MORE WITH TEXT

After completing the following sections, you will be able to take full control over the display of text in your presentations. Specifically, you learn how to customize the use of bullets, edit and organize textual content using the Outline view, and position text on the slide using the Text tool. In terms of formatting guidelines for text, keep in mind the following points as you work through this section:

- Strive for visible and readable text
- Strive for consistency in formatting
- Strive for simplicity and less as more
- Do not mix case (e.g., This Is Difficult To Read On A Slide)
- Do not use too many typefaces
- Avoid writing sentences on your slide; use phrases and summaries
- Ensure parallelism (e.g., consistent use of passive or active voice)

TEXT BULLETS

A bulleted list, as a format, is one technique for controlling and organizing the amount of text displayed on a slide. Bulleted lists are also used to emphasize certain points on a slide. A **bullet** is the graphic (usually a circle) that precedes an item in a list. As you've seen in this learning guide, PowerPoint adds bullets to some placeholders; that is, when you press (**ENTER**) after typing a line of text, a bullet is inserted automatically on the next line.

PowerPoint lets you control the display of bullets and also lets you select custom bullet symbols. You can remove or add bullets to a Text placeholder using the Bullets tool (📃) on the Formatting toolbar. You can also insert custom bullets using the Format, Bullet command. For review, you may want to refer back to Manipulating Bullets in the Adding Slides section of Session 2 before proceeding.

In this section, you change the way bullets appear in the "Chili Cookoff" presentation.

Perform the following steps . . .

1. Display slide 1 of the "Chili Cookoff" presentation in Slide view before proceeding.

2. To use a custom bullet symbol for all slides in your presentation, let's edit the Slide Master. Specifically, let's change the main-level bullets from ■ to ➜. Do the following:
CHOOSE: View, Master, Slide Master

3. CLICK: Master text placeholder (it appears as "Click to edit Master text styles" on the slide)

4. To change the ■ bullet symbol, do the following:
    CHOOSE: Format, Bullet
    CLICK: down arrow beside the *Bullets from* drop-down list box
    SELECT: Wingdings
    (*Note:* You may have to scroll downward to find Wingdings near the bottom of the list.) The Bullet dialog box should look like Figure 3.10.

FIGURE 3.10

BULLET DIALOG BOX,
SHOWING THE
WINGDINGS SYMBOLS

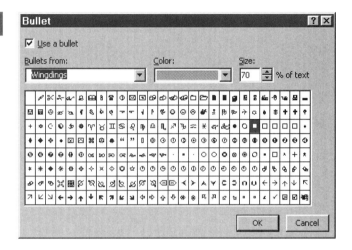

5. To specify a new symbol for the bullet:
    SELECT: ➜
    PRESS: (ENTER) or CLICK: OK

6. To view the slides:
    CLICK: Slide view button (▭)
    Notice that arrows are now used for the major bullet points.

7. To save your changes:
    CLICK: Save button (▣)

QUICK REFERENCE
Changing a Bullet Symbol

1. **Display the Slide Master, or an individual slide.**
2. **Position the insertion point in the line that contains the bullet you want to change.**
3. **CHOOSE: Format, Bullet**
4. **SELECT: a symbol font from the *Bullets from* drop-down list box**
5. **SELECT: a symbol from the Bullet dialog box**
6. **PRESS: (ENTER) or CLICK: OK**

MANIPULATING TEXT IN OUTLINE VIEW

The majority of our time so far has been spent in Slide view and Slide Show view. Many of the tasks you have performed, including changing indent levels and bullets, can also be accomplished using the Outline view. In Outline view, you can apply formatting and reorder your slides. Many people prefer working in Outline view because it lets you see the textual content from more than one slide at a time. Graphics do not display in this mode; there is, however, an icon beside each slide number that indicates whether graphics appear on that slide. The Outlining toolbar, labeled below, appears in Outline view. (*Note:* By default, the Outlining toolbar appears along the left side of the application window.)

Now you will practice using Outline view to move a paragraph and an entire slide.

Perform the following steps . . .

1. Display slide 1 of the "Chili Cookoff" presentation in Slide view.

2. To change the view mode to Outline view:
   CLICK: Outline view button (▤)

3. If the viewing area isn't maximized, maximize the presentation window by clicking its Maximize button (▫). Your screen should now appear similar to Figure 3.11.

FIGURE 3.11

OUTLINE VIEW

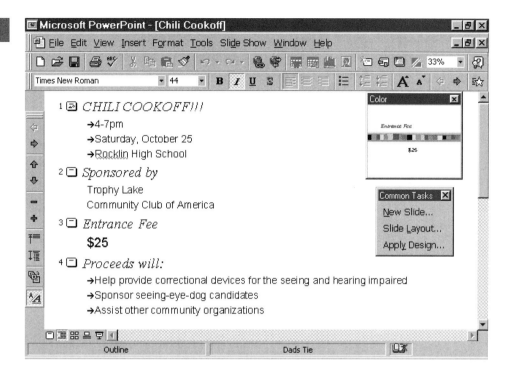

4. To get an overview of the presentation, display the slide titles only:
CLICK: Collapse All button (▦) on the Outlining toolbar

5. To redisplay all of the text:
CLICK: Expand All button (▦) on the Outlining toolbar

6. In Outline view, if you find the text format distracting, you can easily remove it. Do the following:
CLICK: Show Formatting button (▣) on the Outlining toolbar
Your screen should now appear similar to Figure 3.12.

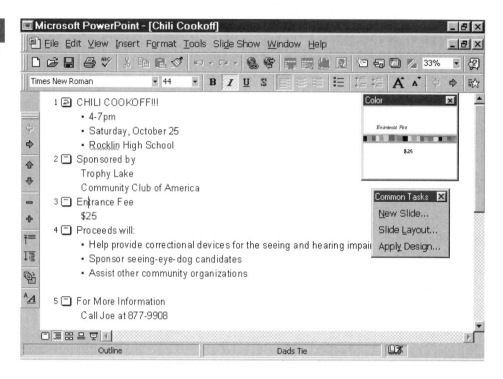

7. To redisplay the formatting:
CLICK: Show Formatting button (⬛) again

8. To select all the text on the first slide so that you can apply additional for-matting, do the following:
CLICK: slide icon for slide 1
When you move the mouse pointer over the icon, it changes to a four-headed arrow (✛).

9. To display the text in bold letters:
CLICK: Bold button (**B**) on the Formatting toolbar

10. To select an individual line or bullet of text on a slide, you position the four-headed arrow (✛) mouse pointer over the associated bullet and click the left mouse button once. To practice moving a paragraph:
SELECT: "Saturday, October 25" on slide 1

11. To move this item so that it displays first in the list:
CLICK: Move Up button (⬆) on the Outlining toolbar
(*Note:* You can also drag the bullet up or down in the list using the mouse.)

12. Using the mouse:
DRAG: "Rocklin High School" bullet above "4-7pm" on slide 1

13. On your own, move the bulleted items to their original positions (i.e. time, date, location)

14. To move slide 3 so that it displays after slide 1, you must first select the slide by clicking its slide icon:
SELECT: slide 3

15. DRAG: slide 3 icon to after slide 1
(*Note:* A horizontal line marks where the slide will be positioned. Ensure that this line is below slide 1 before you release the mouse button. If you make a mistake, choose Edit, Undo and then retry.)

16. On your own, move slide 2 back to its original position after slide 3.

17. Return to Slide view before proceeding to the next section.

IN ADDITION EXPORTING A POWERPOINT OUTLINE TO WORD

1. CHOOSE: File, Send To
   CHOOSE: Microsoft Word

2. SELECT: Outline only in the
   Write-Up dialog box

3. PRESS: (ENTER) or CLICK: OK

USING THE TEXT BOX TOOL

The Title and Text placeholders are great for entering textual content that flows in a consistent and regular fashion. For those other times when you need more flexibility in positioning text on a slide, you use the **Text Box button** (▣) on the Drawing toolbar. Also, you must use the Text Box tool if you want to place text on the Slide Master so that it appears on every slide. You cannot use the Title and Text placeholders on the Slide Master to hold text; they are visible only for changing formatting characteristics.

In this section, you insert free-form text in the bottom right-hand corner of a slide. When you finish, slide 3 of the "Chili Cookoff" presentation will look like Figure 3.13.

FIGURE 3.13

FREE-FORM TEXT PLACED
ON SLIDE 3 OF THE
"CHILI COOKOFF"
PRESENTATION

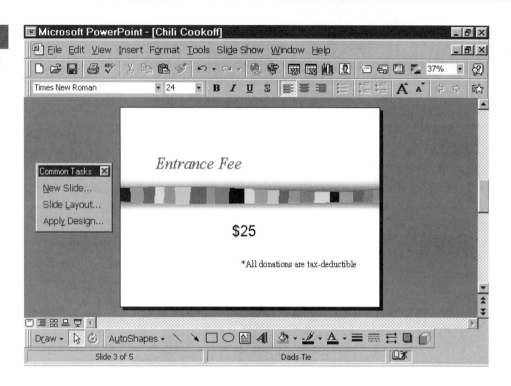

 **Perform the following steps . . .**

1. In Slide view, display slide 3 of the "Chili Cookoff" presentation.

2. To enter free-form text using the Text Box tool:
   CLICK: Text Box button (▦) on the Drawing toolbar

3. By referring to Figure 3.13:
   CLICK: where you want to type your first character (*)

4. An insertion point appears and starts blinking inside the box. The box will expand as you type. Do the following:
   TYPE: ***All Donations are tax-deductible**

5. CLICK: outside the text box
   Your screen should now appear similar to Figure 3.13. (*Note:* By default, the text that you type using the Text Box tool doesn't automatically wrap to the next line. If you want text to wrap automatically, you must first draw a text box by dragging with the mouse and then type in its contents.)

6. Save the "Chili Cookoff" presentation to your Data Files location.

QUICK REFERENCE
Inserting Text Using the
Text Box Tool

1. **Make the desired slide active in the presentation window.**

2. **CLICK: Text Box button (▦) located on the Drawing toolbar**

3. **CLICK: the left mouse button once to position the insertion point, or**
   DRAG: the mouse pointer on the slide to create a text box

WORKING WITH AUTOSHAPES

When your objective is to emphasize important points or promote audience interest in your presentation, consider adding drawings to your slides from PowerPoint's library of AutoShapes. An **AutoShape** is a ready-made shape that you can insert in your document and then resize and move as necessary. PowerPoint provides the following categories of AutoShapes: (1) lines, (2) connectors, (3) basic shapes, (4) block arrows, (5) flowcharting symbols, (6) stars and banners, and (7) callouts. Next you insert an AutoShape in the "Chili Cookoff" presentation and then edit it to meet your needs.

INSERTING AN AUTOSHAPE

You display a menu of AutoShapes by clicking the AutoShape button (AutoShapes) on the Drawing toolbar. After selecting a shape from the AutoShapes menu, you can do one of two things to insert the AutoShape on a slide.

- If you click on your slide, the AutoShape is inserted in its default size.

- If you drag with the mouse to create an outline for the AutoShape, the AutoShape is inserted according to your specifications.

In either case, selection handles appear around the object. At this point, you can further size and move the AutoShape. You use the same procedure to size and move AutoShapes as you do to edit other types of objects.

Now you will insert an AutoShape on slide 3 of the "Chili Cookoff" presentation.

Perform the following steps . . .

1. Display slide 3 of the "Chili Cookoff" presentation in the presentation window.

2. Before continuing, ensure that the Drawing toolbar appears in the application window.

3. In the next few steps, you insert an arrow on the current slide.
   CLICK: AutoShapes button (AutoShapes) on the Drawing toolbar
   CHOOSE: Block Arrows from the menu
   Your screen should now appear similar to Figure 3.14.

FIGURE 3.14

THE BLOCK ARROWS
AUTOSHAPE MENU

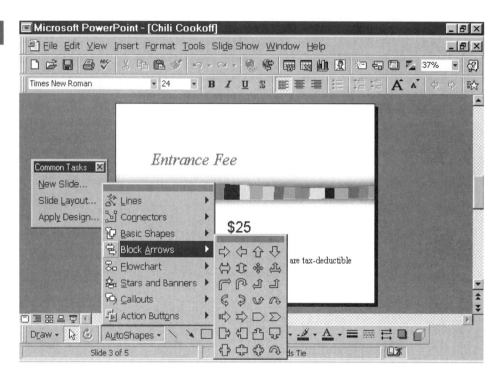

4. CHOOSE: the arrow positioned in the fourth row, second column
The mouse pointer now appears as a cross hair.

5. In this step, you'll insert the AutoShape in its default size.
CLICK: about 1½ inches to the right of "Entrance Fee" title
The arrow now appears on your slide, surrounded by selection handles.
Your screen should now appear similar to Figure 3.15. Don't worry if your
AutoShape is in a different position than the one in Figure 3.15; you resize
and move the AutoShape next.

FIGURE 3.15

A SHAPE WAS INSERTED
IN ITS DEFAULT SIZE

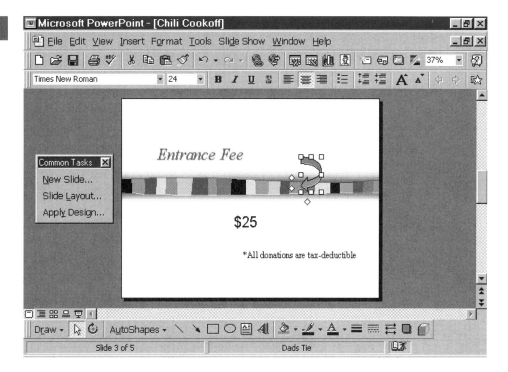

6. If you recall, you resize an object by dragging its sizing handles. You move an object by positioning the mouse pointer over the object until a four-headed arrow (⬌) appears. You then drag the object to its new position. On your own, move and resize the object so that your slide appears similar to the one in Figure 3.16.

7. Save the "Chili Cookoff" presentation to your Data Files location.

FIGURE 3.16

THE SHAPE WAS MOVED
AND RESIZED

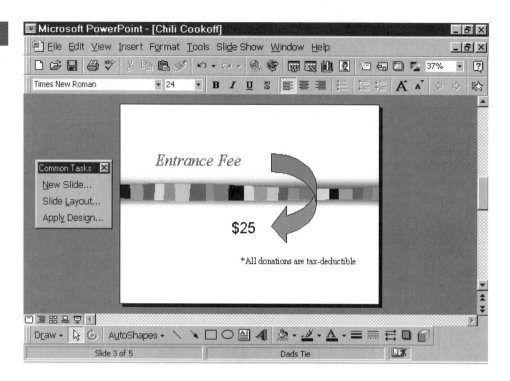

QUICK REFERENCE
Inserting an AutoShape

1. **CLICK: AutoShapes button (AutoShapes) on the Drawing toolbar**
2. **SELECT: an AutoShape category**
3. **SELECT: an AutoShape**
4. **To insert the AutoShape in its default size:**
    CLICK: on the slide, where you want to position the AutoShape
    To insert the AutoShape in the size you specify:
    DRAG: on the slide to create an outline for the AutoShape

---

EDITING AN AUTOSHAPE

In this section, you replace the shape you inserted in the last section with a different shape. You do this by clicking the Draw button (Draw) on the Drawing toolbar, choosing Change AutoShape, and then selecting a different shape. You will then rotate the shape using the Free Rotate button (⟳) on the Drawing toolbar and change the color of the shape using the Fill Color button (◇). Remember that the shape must be selected before you can edit it.

Perform the following steps . . .

1. Ensure that the shape you inserted in the last section is selected.

2. To pick a different shape:
    CLICK: Draw button (Draw)
    CHOOSE: Change AutoShape from the menu
    CHOOSE: Block Arrows
    CHOOSE: the arrow positioned in the first row, fourth column
    Your screen should now appear similar to Figure 3.17.

FIGURE 3.17

CHANGING THE CURRENT
SHAPE

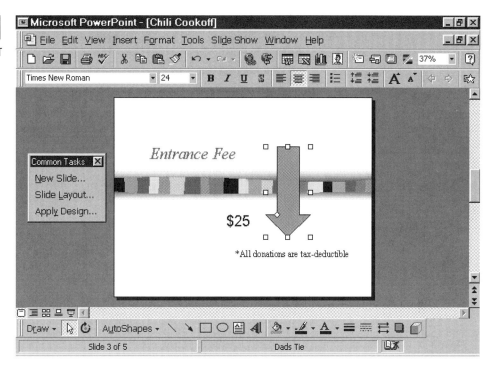

3. Now you will use the Free Rotate button (⟳) to rotate the shape to the left.
   CLICK: Free Rotate button (⟳)
   A round dot appears at each corner of the shape.

4. To rotate the shape, point to the dot on the bottom-left corner of the shape
   and then drag to the left and up. Use Figure 3.18 as your reference. (*Note:*
   After rotating the shape, you may find it necessary to move the shape further away from the dollar amount.)

FIGURE 3.18

ROTATING THE CURRENT
SHAPE

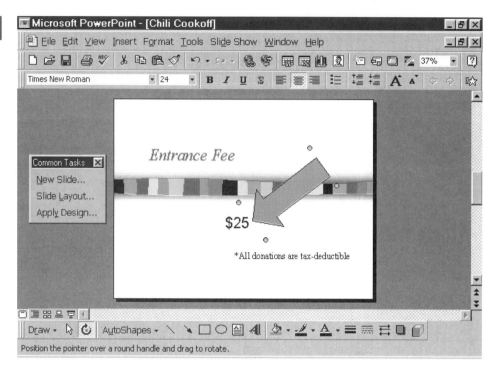

5. Now let's change the color of the arrow.
    CLICK: the arrow on the Fill Color button (⬛▾)
    CLICK: purple (or the color of your choice)
    The shape should appear with the new color.

6. Save the "Chili Cookoff" presentation to your Data Files location.

7. As you can see, you have significant control over how shapes appear in
    your presentation. On your own, practice using some of the other buttons on
    the Drawing toolbar. When you're finished, close the "Chili Cookoff" pre-
    sentation without saving.

QUICK REFERENCE

Selecting a Different
AutoShape

1. **SELECT: the current AutoShape on the slide**

2. **CLICK: Draw button (⬛Draw▾) on the AutoShapes toolbar**

3. **CHOOSE: Change AutoShape**

4. **SELECT: a different AutoShape**

Summary

In this session, you learned how to add your own design flair to a presentation. The session began by describing PowerPoint's templates, which you can use to define how text will appear on a slide, where objects will be positioned, and which colors will be used. You also edited the Slide Master, which holds the formatting specifications for the Title and Text placeholders and the background for the entire presentation. In the second half of the session, you learned the importance of selecting colors for a presentation and how to choose and apply a color scheme. The session concluded by leading you through selecting a custom bullet, manipulating text in the Outline view, and inserting free-form text on a slide using the Text Box tool. You also practiced inserting and editing AutoShapes.

COMMAND SUMMARY

Many of the commands and procedures appearing in this session are provided in Table 3.1 below.

TABLE 3.1	Task Description	Menu Command	Alternative Methods
Command Summary	Apply a new design template	Format, Apply Design Template	Choose Apply Design on the Common Tasks toolbar
	Edit the Title Master	View, Master, Title Master	
	Edit the Slide Master	View, Master, Slide Master	(SHIFT) + ⬜
	Reapply the Slide Master attributes	Format, Slide Layout	Choose Slide Layout on the Common Tasks toolbar
	Change the color scheme	Format, Slide Color Scheme	
	Select a custom bullet symbol	Format, Bullet	
	Reverse the last command executed	Edit, Undo	↶
	Insert an AutoShape	Insert, Picture, AutoShapes	Click AutoShapes button (AutoShapes ▾) on the Drawing toolbar
	Change the AutoShape		Click Draw button (Draw ▾) on the Drawing toolbar and then choose Change AutoShape
	Rotate an AutoShape		↻ (Drawing toolbar)
	Change the color of an AutoShape		♦▾ (Drawing toolbar)

KEY TERMS

AutoShape
In PowerPoint, a ready-made shape that you can customize to meet your needs.

bullet
A graphic that precedes an item in a list.

color scheme
In PowerPoint, a set of eight colors that are used as the main colors in your presentation.

Handout Master
In PowerPoint, this slide holds the formatting specifications for the headers and footers of all Handout pages.

Notes Master
In PowerPoint, this slide holds the formatting specifications for the placeholders and background of all Notes pages.

Slide Master
In PowerPoint, this slide holds the formatting specifications for the placeholders and background of all slides except Title slides.

Title Master
In PowerPoint, this slide holds the formatting specifications for the placeholders and background of all Title slides.

Text Box button
This button is available on the Drawing toolbar and lets you enter text on a slide without using the placeholders.

EXERCISES

SHORT ANSWER

1. For what reason might you want to use Black and White view?

2. What is the procedure for typing text outside the current placeholders on a slide?

3. What are the advantages of working in Outline view?

4. How is your presentation affected when you choose Apply Design from the Common Tasks toolbar and then select a design?

5. Why is it significant that changes you make to individual slides are considered *exceptions* to the Slide Master?

6. In Outline View, how do you select all the text on a slide?

7. In Outline View, how do you move a slide?

8. When would you use the Bullet On/Off button?

9. When would you want to use the Title Master instead of the Slide Master?

10. What procedure would you use to change the color of an AutoShape?

HANDS-ON

(*Note:* Ensure that you know the location of your Advantage Files and where to store your Data Files. If necessary, ask your instructor or lab assistant for additional information.)

1. In this exercise, you retrieve the "CityNews" presentation from your Advantage Files location and then edit the Slide Master, change the design template, insert a clip art image, and apply a different color scheme.

   a. Retrieve "CityNews" from the Advantage Files location.

   b. Using the Slide Master, modify the presentation so that the title and main text of every slide appear bold.

   c. Using the Slide Master, select a new custom bullet symbol (■) to replace the main bullet symbol (●).

   d. Apply the "Zesty" design template to the presentation.

   e. Edit slide 5 of the presentation to look like Figure 3.19. (*Hint:* The clip image was resized and moved, and the text placeholder on the left was enlarged.)

FIGURE 3.19

SLIDE 5 OF THE
"CITYNEWS"
PRESENTATION

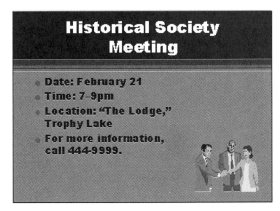

   f. Edit the current color scheme. Select a color scheme that uses a white background. Apply the new color scheme to the entire presentation.

   g. Display the presentation using Slide Show view.

   h. Return to Slide view.

   i. To reverse the color change you made in Step f, choose Edit, Undo from the Menu bar.

   j. Save the presentation as "Trophy Lake News" to your Data Files location.

   k. Close the presentation.

2. In this exercise, you edit the "Trophy Lake News" presentation that you saved in exercise 1.

    a. Ensure that slide 6 of the "Trophy Lake News" presentation appears on your screen.

    b. Using the Text Box button (🖾), insert the following text in the bottom right-hand corner of slide 6:
        `*All pets must be leashed`

    c. Change the size of the newly inserted text to 20 points.

    d. Change the font of the newly inserted text to Arial, if this font exists on your computer.

    e. Display the presentation in Outline view.

    f. On slide 2, move the "Historical Society" bullet after the "Jazz Festival" bullet.

    g. Move slide 5 (Historical Society) to after slide 6 (Jazz Festival).

    h. Display the presentation using Slide view.

    i. Edit slide 4 to look like Figure 3.20. (*Hint:* Insert the shapes from the "Stars and Banners" AutoShape category. Use their default size. Drag the shapes into position.)

FIGURE 3.20

SLIDE 4 OF THE "TROPHY LAKE NEWS" PRESENTATION

    j. Display the entire presentation, beginning with slide 1, in Slide Show view.

    k. Save the presentation as "Trophy Lake News" to your Data Files location.

    l. Close the presentation.

3. In this exercise, you open a presentation called "Messy" from the Advantage Files location and improve its design. In its current form the presentation contains too many elements, thus confusing the message.

    a. Open "Messy" from the Advantage Files location.

    b. Delete all the AutoShapes on slide 1.

   c.   Change the bullets from ➜ to ● on slides 2 and 3. (*Hint:* Use the Slide Master.)

   d.   Apply the Bulleted List layout to slide 3.

   e.   Change the font size of the bulleted text on slides 2 and 3 to 28 point.

   f.   Choose a different design for the presentation.

   g.   Save the presentation as "Tidy" to your Data Files location.

4.   On your own, create a presentation that contains the information and topics we describe below. Keep the following in mind as you proceed:

   a.   We've underlined the suggested title for each slide. However, feel free to modify or add to the topics we describe below.

   b.   Decide which design template and layouts to use to best present the information.

   c.   Enhance your presentation with one or more AutoShapes and clip art images.

   d.   Ensure that your name and the current date appear on the bottom of each slide. (*Hint:* Use the Slide Master and the Text Box tool.)

   e.   When you are finished, save the presentation as "On Your Own-3" to your Data Files location.

       <u>The Structure of the United States Government</u>
       by
       your name

       <u>The Three Branches of Government</u>
       Executive Branch
       Legislative Branch
       Judicial Branch

       <u>Executive Branch</u>
       The President
       The Vice President

       <u>Legislative Branch</u>
       Congress
          ● *Senate*
          ● *House*

       <u>Judicial Branch</u>
       The Supreme Court of the United States

5.   On your own, create a presentation that tries to convince your audience (a relative, business associate, or other individual) why you need a vacation. Use your experience with PowerPoint to make the most compelling case possible. When you're finished, save the presentation as "On Your Own-4" to your Data Files location. (Bon Voyage!)

H2 UNDERSCAPING LTD.

(*Note:* In the following case problems, assume the role of the primary characters and perform the same steps that they identify. You may want to re-read the session opening.)

1. By his next lunch meeting with Vi Krieg, Chip had already developed a storyboard for his presentation. "A storyboard," he explained to Vi, "reduces the amount of wasted time typically spent brainstorming around the computer. I simply jot down everything that I want to show on each slide in these little boxes. It's a great way to organize my thoughts for a presentation." Vi was very impressed with the page Chip handed to her (an example of which appears below.)

Title: Business Show, 1996 **#1** **Sub-title:** Presented by Chip Yee H2 UnderScaping Ltd.	**Title:** Evening's Agenda **#2** **Bullets:** • Chamber's mission • Benefits of membership • Community affairs • Member profile • Summary
Title: Chamber's Mission **#3** **Bullets:** • To lobby for changes in law to promote economic prosperity for all • To work for opportunity and education for small businesses nationwide • To promote the policies and initiatives of the National Chambers of Commerce	**Title:** Benefits of Membership **#4** **Bullets:** • Business-to-business directory • Monthly luncheon meetings • Monthly newsletter • Corporate library • Special events and guest speakers
Title: Community Affairs **#5** **Bullets:** • High-school career prep program • Organizer of celebrity auction for children's charities • Organizer of downtown Easter parade • Fund-raiser for local women's center	**Title:** Member Profile **#6** **Bullets:** Donna Osaki, M.D., is off to Saudi Arabia to set up the country's first community health center. Donna accepted this position immediately when approached by the Surgeon General. We wish Donna the very best overseas!
Title: Summary **#7** **Bullets:** • Our Chamber is true to its ideals • Our Chamber works for its members • Our Chamber works for its community • Our Chamber has the best people!	**Title:** Closing **#8** **Sub-title:** Thank you for attending this evening!

"Are you sure we can pull this off using a computer-based presentation?" asked Vi, wondering if Chip realized the actual time and effort it would involve. Chip nodded confidently. "You see, Vi, I've already planned out how this will work on the computer. First, I'll take my storyboard and create an on-screen presentation using the Contemporary template since it communicates a dignified and professional image for the Chamber. Next, I'll position your name as our Chamber president in the bottom right-hand corner of each slide using the Text Box button on the Slide Master. Everything will look just stunning!

Vi was getting excited about Chip's plans for the presentation. She couldn't wait to see the final product and begged Chip to send her a printed copy of his work as soon as he was finished. Chip agreed, and they departed from their lunch feeling well-nourished and anticipating a wonderful Business Show!

Save this presentation as "Business Show" to your Data Files location.

2. Two weeks before he was to make his Chamber presentation, Chip received a letter from Ms. Paula Deviq, a business administration teacher at the local high school. The letter read, *"Dear Mr. Yee, I understand that you are preparing a presentation for the Chamber at this year's Business Show banquet. I have a proposition for you. I would like you to deliver your presentation to my senior class in business administration early next week. In return, you would enjoy an opportunity to practice your speech and receive constructive criticism from my class. Please consider this invitation and reply to me as soon as possible. Sincerely, Paula Deviq."* Chip called Paula immediately after reading the letter and accepted her polite, and timely, invitation.

Thinking about the presentation for Paula's class that evening, Chip decided that he should change the look and feel of the presentation to better suit high school students. Instead of using the look of the Contemporary template, he decided to pick something much livelier and more colorful to keep their attention. Also, he would look through the Clip Gallery to find some relevant pictures. Specifically, he wanted to add three different pictures—on each of slides 4, 5, and 6. Another change he would make would be to select custom bullet symbols, perhaps ♣ or ☽. Lastly, Chip would remove Vi Krieg's name from the Slide Master and replace it with his favorite quote, "Do what you love and the money will follow!" All of these changes would take some time, but he knew the payoff would be worth the effort.

Once finished, Chip proceeded through a dry run of his presentation using the Slide Show view. Happy with the results, he saved the presentation as "School Presentation 1" to the Data Files location.

3. Chip arrived at the high school 30 minutes early for his presentation. He was just opening the front door to the school when he was greeted by a well-dressed woman in her mid-thirties. "Mr. Yee, I presume?" Chip smiled and extended his hand to the teacher. "Yes, I hope I'm not too early for your class, Ms. Deviq?" "Oh, no, no . . . but we've experienced a small technical problem this morning with our A.V. system. I'm afraid we won't be able to connect your laptop computer to an LCD projection panel. I was hoping that you could print out your presentation onto black-and-white overheads using my laser printer. I'm sorry to make you deliver your presentation the old-fashioned way, but I'm sure my students would enjoy it all the same."

    Chip immediately began rehearsing the procedure in his mind. He would have to change his template from an on-screen presentation to a black and white overhead presentation. He would display the presentation in black and white and then review it on-screen to see how the objects looked. Realizing that he had been staring at Paula and saying nothing for the past ten seconds, Chip apologized and assured her that it was not a problem to convert his presentation to overheads. He then asked to be shown to her office to begin the process.

    Save this presentation as "School Presentation 2" to your Data Files location.

4. Back at his office, Chip received an official "Invitation to Quote" from the federal government. The government is nearing completion on a million-dollar expansion of their administration wing and requires landscaping services to be completed for their opening next month. Each vendor is being asked to prepare a 15-minute presentation on their company's strengths and present it to the selection committee this coming Monday.

    Using the storyboards shown below, Chip completed the handwritten version of the presentation. Unfortunately, he had to fly to Denver on family business and could not finish converting the presentation to PowerPoint. As his office assistant, you must now take Chip's storyboards and create a presentation appropriate for the federal government's selection committee, complete with introduction and closing slides. Chip also mentioned that you should choose templates, color schemes, typefaces, clip art, and AutoShapes for the presentation. Good luck!

Introduction	#1	Company Background	#2
(Remember to put the title of the presentation, my name, and the company's name on this slide!)		Started in 1992 by Mr. Chip Yee, H2U has become an innovator in the business of underground sprinkler systems.	
Why We Are the Best	#3	Partial Client List	#4
The Most-Talented Designers The Most-Dedicated Staff The Most-Current Technology The Most-Satisfied Clients!		Mount Rushmore Society New Jersey Turnpike Assoc. Yasgusa's Farm, Inc. Willy's Motor Inn, Route 66	
Summary	#5	Closing Slide	#6
(Remember to put a summary of the presentation here.)		(Remember to thank them for attending the presentation and provide time for questions.)	

Save the presentation as "Federal Government" to your Data Files location.

Microsoft PowerPoint 97 for Windows

Adding Visual Effects

SESSION

4

HTTP://WWW

IRWIN

COMPUTER & INFORMATION TECHNOLOGY

SESSION OUTLINE

Working with Objects
Inserting Clip Art
Inserting Pictures
Creating Graphs
Creating Organizational Charts
Designing an Electronic Slide Show
Summary
Key Terms
Exercises

INTRODUCTION

PowerPoint provides you with powerful graphic and visual support, which makes it relatively easy to add professional touches to your presentations. In this session, we show you how to work with many kinds of visual objects including clip art images, graphs, and organizational charts. In addition, we lead you through adding special effects to your electronic presentations.

IMMACULATE PERCEPTIONS, INC.

"Creating a memorable corporate identity for all of our clients!" screamed the black letters on a bright yellow sign. This sign did not appear on a billboard, or even on a bus stop bench; it was placed dead center over the reception desk for Immaculate Perceptions, Inc. (IPI), a young and striving advertising agency in Brandon, Oregon. Started in 1991 as a partnership between Connie Appleton and Bobbie Brukowski, IPI now specializes in providing customers with marketing and advertising materials for trade shows and point-of-purchase (POP) displays.

Last week, Bobbie introduced the company's creative staff to Microsoft PowerPoint as a vehicle for communicating their clients' images and as a possible source of revenue. "It's great!" exclaimed Bobbie, pacing around the boardroom table. "You can add pictures and clip art, create graphs of financial and statistical information, and even match the presentation to their corporate colors. And the best part is that you can create a self-running slide show for use at a trade show booth—they don't even have to be present!" The staff was very receptive to Bobbie's pitch. Connie, who had listened to every word but had not spoken until this point, summarized the meeting with "Let's find out as much as we can about PowerPoint's visual tools and then meet again on Monday to discuss its uses for the upcoming Computer and Communications Show at the Shoreline Center. Remember, learn as much as you can about PowerPoint in the next week!"

WORKING WITH OBJECTS

Microsoft provides several Office tools, or **mini-apps,** that can be used by PowerPoint. These mini-apps enable you to create objects that may be embedded into a presentation. To find out which mini-apps are available to you, choose the Insert, Object command from the menu and then browse through the list of objects that appears in the dialog box. You may also see the names of other software applications such as CorelDRAW!, depending on which applications you have installed on your computer. The Insert Object dialog box lists all the programs on your computer for which you may insert output, such as a drawing object from CorelDRAW!, into your PowerPoint presentation.

Although not all of these may be installed on your computer, Microsoft's mini-apps include the following:

Clip Gallery   Enables you to select and insert clip art from a library of cataloged images. For example:

Equation Editor   Enables you to create complex equations using special math symbols and typesetting standards. For example:

$$\sigma^2 = \frac{\sum\limits_{i=1}^{N}(X_i - \mu)^2}{N}$$

Graph   Enables you to easily insert a graph into your document without having to launch Excel. For example:

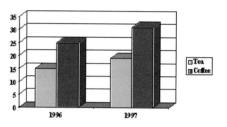

Organization Chart   Enables you to design, build, and insert an organization chart into your document. For example:

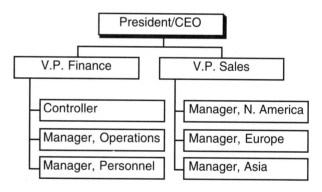

WordArt   Allows you to apply special effects to textual information in your document. (*Note:* This mini-app has been integrated into Microsoft Office so it doesn't appear in the list in the Insert Object dialog box.)

For further information on inserting and manipulating objects, refer to the In Addition boxes that appear throughout this guide and to the *Integrating Microsoft Office 97* Student Learning Guide in the Advantage Series for Computer Education.

INSERTING CLIP ART

A picture is worth a thousand words! Although this phrase is overused, its truth is undeniable. Graphics add personality to your presentation and convey information more efficiently than text alone. Unfortunately, many new computer users struggle with the tendency to place too many graphics on a single screen. To assist your planning of how and when to use graphics, apply these basic principles: strive for simplicity, use emphasis sparingly, and ensure a visual balance between graphics and text. Fortunately, PowerPoint's AutoLayouts already encourage a balanced and visually appealing use of graphics.

The Microsoft Clip Gallery provides a one-stop shopping mall for all your clip art images. You worked with clip art in Session 2 when you chose the "Text & Clip Art" AutoLayout. PowerPoint provides the following additional methods for inserting a clip art image on a slide:

- CLICK: Insert Clip Art button (⬚) on the Standard toolbar
- CHOOSE: Insert, Picture, Clip Art from the menu
- CHOOSE: Insert, Object from the menu and select Microsoft Clip Gallery from the dialog box

In the following sections, you use the Insert Clip Art button (⬚) on the Standard toolbar and then format and edit the image using the Picture toolbar.

INSERTING A CLIP ART IMAGE

Now you will insert an image from the Clip Gallery.

Perform the following steps . . .

1. Open "Software" from the Advantage Files location and then review the contents of the presentation in Slide Show view.

2. Ensure that slide 1 of the "Software" presentation appears in Slide view.

3. Let's use the Insert Clip Art button (⬚) to insert a clip art image on this slide.
   CLICK: Insert Clip Art button (⬚)
   The Clip Gallery dialog box appears.

4. SELECT: Shapes from the list of categories on the left
   SELECT: the image shown in Figure 4.1 from the area on the right
   CLICK: Insert button
   Your screen should now appear similar to Figure 4.1. The image currently covers up the text on the slide. Notice that the Picture toolbar appears. Whenever a clip art image or picture is selected, the Picture toolbar appears so that you can edit the image, if necessary.

FIGURE 4.1

SLIDE 1 OF THE
"SOFTWARE"
PRESENTATION

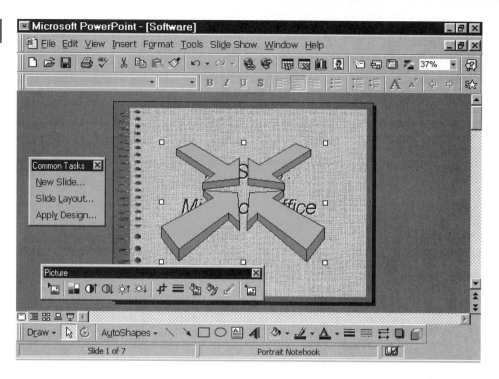

5. Let's experiment with moving the clip art image to behind the text on this slide. To do this, the image must be selected. While pointing to the clip art image on the slide:
RIGHT-CLICK: to display the shortcut menu
CHOOSE: Order

6. Since the clip art image is the currently selected object, the command you choose now will affect the clip art image.
CHOOSE: Send to Back
The clip art image now appears behind the slide's text (Figure 4.2).

FIGURE 4.2

THE IMAGE WAS
MOVED TO BEHIND
THE TEXT

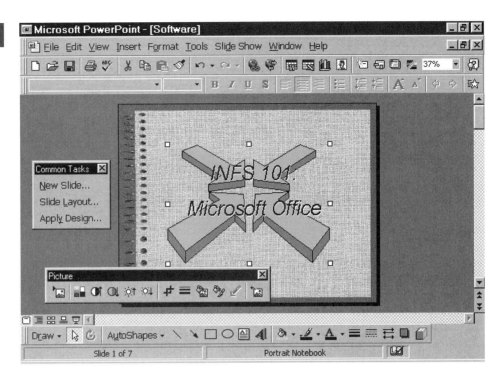

7. At this point, the text is somewhat difficult to read. If we increase the brightness of the image, the dark letters in the title may stand out more. To do this, you will use More Brightness button (⊡) on the Picture toolbar. Before continuing, ensure that the clip art image is still selected.
   CLICK: More Brightness button (⊡) about ten times

8. The text should be easier to see, but let's now add the bold attribute to the title text. First you must select the Title placeholder.
   CLICK: any letter in the title
   The Title placeholder should now be selected.

9. To change the formatting of the title:
   CHOOSE: Edit, Select All
   CLICK: Bold button (**B**)

10. CLICK: outside the Title placeholder
    Your screen should now appear similar to Figure 4.3.

FIGURE 4.3

THE TITLE TEXT IS
EASIER TO READ

11. Save the presentation as "INFS 101" to your Data Files location.

QUICK REFERENCE
Changing the Order of
Slide Objects

1. **SELECT: the object you want to move**
2. **RIGHT-CLICK: to display the shortcut menu**
3. **CHOOSE: Order**
   CHOOSE: an option from the menu

QUICK REFERENCE
Changing the Brightness
Level of an Image

1. **SELECT: the object you want to edit**
2. **On the Picture toolbar:**
   CLICK: More Brightness button ( ), or
   CLICK: Less Brightness button ( )

IN ADDITION INSERTING MOVIES AND SOUNDS

You can insert movies and audio
tracks for playback from within your
presentation using the Insert, Movies
and Sounds command. To play
back the video clip or sound, display

the presentation in Slide Show view and then click
on the object.

INSERTING PICTURES

In addition to clip art images, you can insert graphic files into your presentation. A computer **graphic file** is usually created by an artist, designer, or desktop publisher. However, you can easily create your own graphic files if you have access to a **scanner.** A scanner is a hardware device that converts photographs and other paper-based material into computer images. Just as a photocopier makes a representation from paper to paper, a scanner makes a copy from paper to computer. You can insert an image directly from your scanner using the Insert, Picture, From Scanner command. Or, if you save the image to disk, you can insert the image file into your presentation using the Insert, Picture, From File command.

QUICK REFERENCE
Inserting Graphics

1. **Position the insertion point where you want to insert the object.**
2. **CHOOSE: Insert, Picture, From Scanner, or**
   CHOOSE: Insert, Picture, From File

CREATING GRAPHS

Most people recognize the benefit of using graphics to improve their effectiveness in communicating information. Clearly, a chart or graph is easier to decipher than rows and columns of tiny numbers. Fortunately, PowerPoint makes it relatively easy for you to include graphs in your presentations. It comes with a powerful supplementary program called **Microsoft Graph.** The Microsoft Graph 97 mini-app helps you produce great-looking charts and graphs—right from within PowerPoint! Graph does not replace a full-featured spreadsheet application like Microsoft Excel, but it does provide a more convenient tool for embedding simple charts into presentations.

There are a variety of methods for adding a graph to a slide (concentrate on using the first two).

- CLICK: Insert Chart button () on the Standard toolbar
- DOUBLE-CLICK: graph placeholder on an AutoLayout slide
- CHOOSE: Insert, Chart from the Menu bar
- CHOOSE: Insert, Object from the Menu bar and select Microsoft Graph from the dialog box

In this section, you add a graph to a slide.

Perform the following steps . . .

1. Ensure that the "INFS 101" presentation appears in the presentation window and that the Common Tasks toolbar appears.

2. Display the last slide in the presentation (slide 7) by dragging the elevator scroll box to the bottom of the vertical scroll bar.

3. To insert a new slide:
   CHOOSE: New Slide from the Common Tasks toolbar

4. In the Slide Layout dialog box:
   SELECT: Chart layout

5. To display the slide:
   PRESS: (ENTER) or CLICK: OK
   Your screen should now appear similar to Figure 4.4.

FIGURE 4.4

SLIDE 7 WITH THE
PLACEHOLDERS VISIBLE

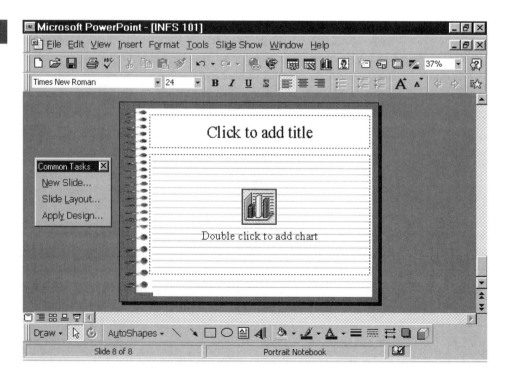

6. CLICK: Title placeholder
   TYPE: **HOW YOU'RE GRADED**

7. To insert a graph:
   DOUBLE-CLICK: the graph placeholder
   The Graph datasheet appears in a separate window with sample information. Similarly to using an electronic spreadsheet, you add and edit data in the datasheet that you want to plot on a graph. Figure 4.5 shows the datasheet as it first appears and how it will look after you edit it.

FIGURE 4.5

EDITING THE DATASHEET

Before

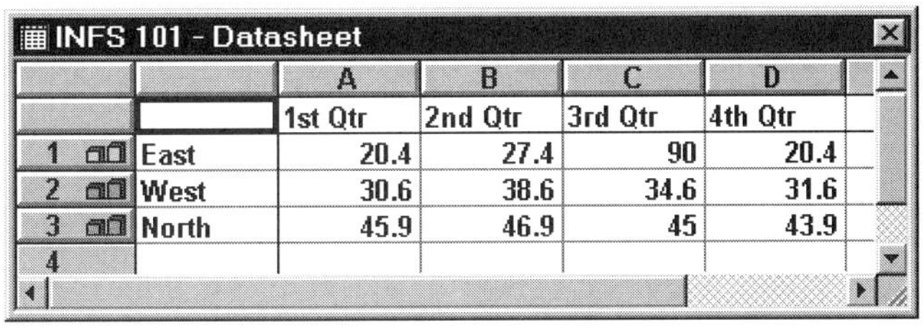

INFS 101 - Datasheet		A	B	C	D	
		1st Qtr	2nd Qtr	3rd Qtr	4th Qtr	
1	East	20.4	27.4	90	20.4	
2	West	30.6	38.6	34.6	31.6	
3	North	45.9	46.9	45	43.9	
4						

After

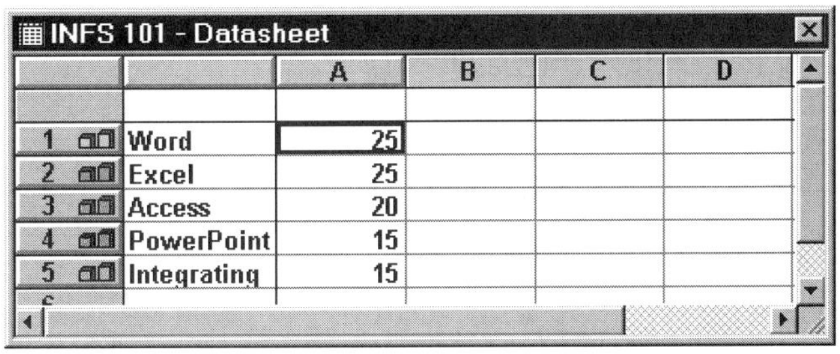

INFS 101 - Datasheet		A	B	C	D	
1	Word	25				
2	Excel	25				
3	Access	20				
4	PowerPoint	15				
5	Integrating	15				
6						

8. In this step, you delete all the data that currently appears in the datasheet. To do this, you first select the entire datasheet by clicking the upper-left corner of the datasheet, directly below the Title bar. You then press the **DELETE** key.
   CLICK: the upper-left corner of the datasheet (refer to Figure 4.6)
   PRESS: **DELETE**

FIGURE 4.6

DELETING THE
CONTENTS OF THE
DATASHEET

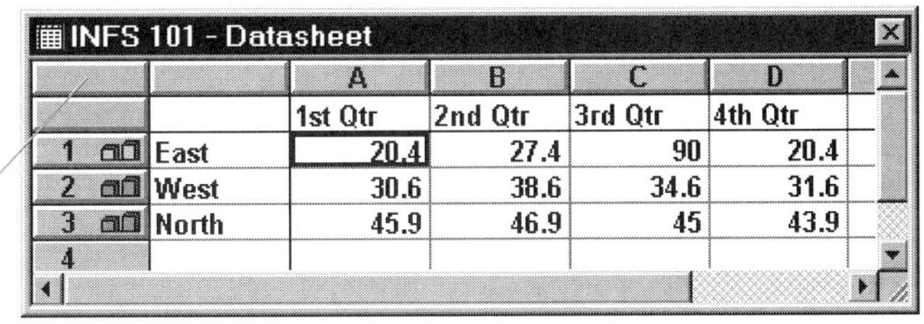

Click here to
select all the
cells in the
datasheet

INFS 101 - Datasheet		A	B	C	D	
		1st Qtr	2nd Qtr	3rd Qtr	4th Qtr	
1	East	20.4	27.4	90	20.4	
2	West	30.6	38.6	34.6	31.6	
3	North	45.9	46.9	45	43.9	
4						

9. To enter data into the datasheet, you click the cross hair mouse pointer on the appropriate *cell* (the intersection of a row and a column) in the datasheet. In this step, you enter the titles.
CLICK: in the cell to the right of the number 1
TYPE: Word
PRESS: ENTER
The cursor automatically moves to the cell below.
TYPE: Excel
PRESS: ENTER
TYPE: Access
PRESS: ENTER
TYPE: PowerPoint
PRESS: ENTER
TYPE: Integrating
PRESS: ENTER

10. Now you prepare to enter the data.
PRESS: CTRL + HOME
The cursor automatically moves to where you will type in the first value (25).

11. To enter the data:
TYPE: 25
PRESS: ENTER
TYPE: 25
PRESS: ENTER
TYPE: 20
PRESS: ENTER
TYPE: 15
PRESS: ENTER
TYPE: 15
PRESS: ENTER
If you drag the bottom border of the datasheet downward and then press CTRL + HOME, the datasheet should appear similar to the completed datasheet in Figure 4.5. (*Note:* Some of the headings may be obscured in your datasheet.)

12. Let's now display the graph on the slide:
CLICK: anywhere in the background of the presentation window
The graph is inserted automatically into your presentation. Your screen should now appear similar to Figure 4.7.

FIGURE 4.7

THE GRAPH IS
INSERTED ON THE SLIDE

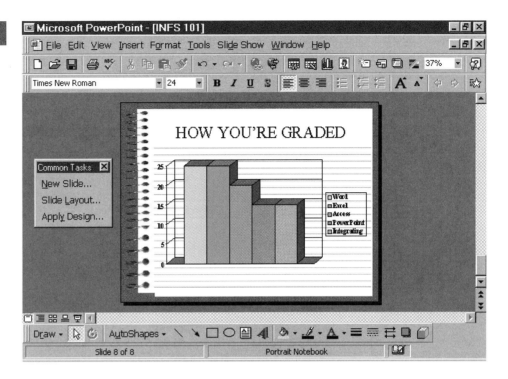

13. Save the presentation as "INFS 101" to your Data Files location.

Once you've inserted a graph on a slide, you can edit it at any time by double-clicking the image on the slide to load Microsoft Graph. While displaying a presentation in Slide view, you use the same techniques for sizing and moving a graph as you use for manipulating other types of objects.

QUICK REFERENCE	● **CLICK: Insert Chart button (⊞) on the Standard toolbar**
Inserting a Graph	● **DOUBLE-CLICK: graph placeholder on an AutoLayout slide**
	● **CHOOSE: Insert, Chart from the menu**
	● **CHOOSE: Insert, Object and then select Microsoft Graph**

IN ADDITION INSERTING AN EXCEL WORKSHEET

1. CLICK: Insert Microsoft Excel Worksheet button (⊞) on the Standard toolbar

2. Use the mouse to outline the dimensions of the worksheet in the pull-down menu.

3. Edit the worksheet object using Excel's commands and procedures.

4. Resize and move the object as necessary.

IN ADDITION INSERTING A WORD TABLE

1. CLICK: Insert Microsoft Word Table button (▦) on the Standard toolbar

2. Use the mouse to outline the dimensions of the table in the pull-down menu.

3. Edit the table object using Word's commands and procedures.

4. Resize and move the object as necessary.

CREATING ORGANIZATIONAL CHARTS

Microsoft Organization Chart allows you to create organization charts and other hierarchical diagrams. Similarly to working with graphics, you apply the principles of simplicity, emphasis, and balance to creating **organization charts.** In the following steps, you will insert a simple organizational chart into the "INFS 101" presentation.

There are a few methods for inserting an organization chart on a slide.

- DOUBLE-CLICK: organization chart placeholder on an AutoLayout slide

- CHOOSE: Insert, Picture, Organization Chart from the Menu bar

In this section, you add an organization chart to a slide.

Perform the following steps . . .

1. Ensure that slide 8 of the "INFS 101" presentation appears in the presentation window.

2. To insert a new slide:
   CHOOSE: New Slide from the Common Tasks toolbar

3. To select the Organization Chart AutoLayout slide:
   SELECT: Organization Chart layout
   PRESS: (ENTER) or CLICK: OK
   Your screen should now appear similar to Figure 4.8.

FIGURE 4.8

ORGANIZATION CHART
PLACEHOLDER ON A
NEW SLIDE

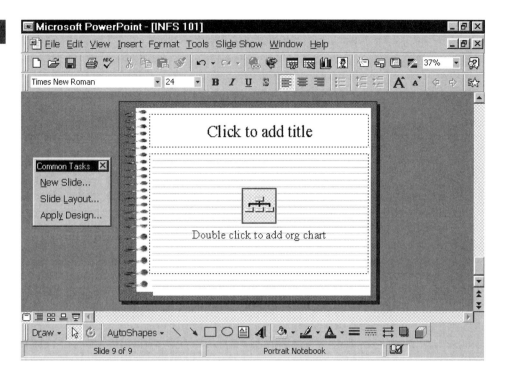

4. CLICK: Title placeholder
TYPE: **NEED HELP?**

5. To insert an organization chart:
DOUBLE-CLICK: the organization chart placeholder
You should see four boxes on the screen; the topmost box should already be selected.

6. To edit the content of the organization chart boxes:
TYPE: **Maria D. Perez**
PRESS: **ENTER**
TYPE: **Lead Instructor**

7. CLICK: the far left box, located in the second row of the chart
TYPE: **Feliberto Reyes**
PRESS: **ENTER**
TYPE: **Assistant Instructor**

8. CLICK: the box in the center of the second row
TYPE: **Frank Rogers**
PRESS: **ENTER**
TYPE: **Lab Assistant**

9. CLICK: the box on the right of the second row
TYPE: `Maritza James`
PRESS: (ENTER)
TYPE: `Lab Assistant`

10. To add a new box to the chart:
CLICK: Subordinate button (Subordinate: ⌐) in the toolbar
CLICK: Maria D. Perez' box
A new box appears on the second level.

11. Because the new box is already selected, do the following:
TYPE: `Roxanna Adams`
PRESS: (ENTER)
TYPE: `Network Manager`
CLICK: anywhere outside of the chart to remove the active selection
The Microsoft Organization Chart window should now appear similar to
Figure 4.9.

FIGURE 4.9

THE COMPLETED
ORGANIZATION CHART

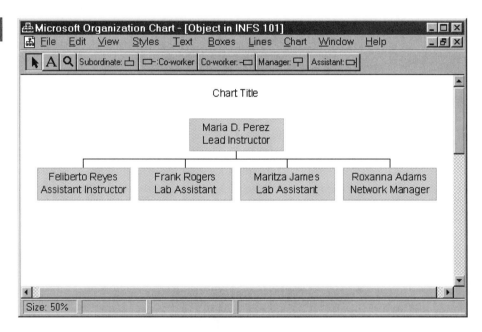

12. To return to PowerPoint and update the slide:
CHOOSE: File, Exit and Return to INFS 101
(*CAUTION:* Choose the command from the Microsoft Organization Chart
Menu bar and not the PowerPoint Menu bar.)

13. CLICK: Yes command button to update the presentation
The organization chart should now appear on the slide.

14. On your own, you may want to select the organization chart object and
enlarge it by dragging its top border upward. The chart's text may be easier
to read.

15. Save the "INFS 101" presentation to your Data Files location.

Once you've inserted an organization chart on a slide, you can edit it at any time by double-clicking the image on the slide to load Microsoft Organization Chart. You may, for example, decide to change the box colors, border color, border style, and so on. While displaying a presentation in Slide view, you use the same techniques for sizing and moving an organization chart image as you used for manipulating other types of objects.

QUICK REFERENCE	● **DOUBLE-CLICK: organization chart placeholder on an AutoLayout slide**
Inserting an Organization Chart	● **CHOOSE: Insert, Picture, Organization Chart from the Menu bar**

IN ADDITION COPYING AND MOVING BETWEEN MICROSOFT OFFICE APPLICATIONS

1. Select the text, data, or other object that you want to copy. Then click the Cut button (🖾) or the Copy button (🖾).

2. Switch to the application you want to move or copy into and then position the cursor.

3. Click the Paste button (🖾) to insert the contents of the Clipboard at the cursor location. (*Note:* If you choose Edit, Paste Special from the Menu bar and then choose the Paste Link option, the pasted information will be linked to its source application. Any changes you make to the data in the source application will show up in the linked application.)

DESIGNING AN ELECTRONIC SLIDE SHOW

So far in this learning guide, you've viewed a slide show using PowerPoint's default settings. No transitions between slides or timed pauses have been added to Slide Show view. In the following sections, you learn how to take control of your electronic presentations by setting timings, adding transitions, creating build slides, and adding animation. You also learn how to customize a slide show for a specific audience.

SETTING TIMINGS

Timing refers to the amount of time a slide stays on the screen during Slide Show view. Timing is especially useful for those occasions when you want to let a presentation run unattended in a continuous loop. You specify timings for your presentation by choosing the Slide Show, Rehearse Timings command or by clicking the Rehearse New Timings button (🖾) in Slide Sorter view.

In this section, you add timings to the "INFS 101" presentation.

Perform the following steps . . .

1. Ensure that slide 1 of the "INFS 101" presentation appears in the presentation window.

2. To build timings into the slide show:
   CHOOSE: Slide Show, Rehearse Timings from the Menu bar

3. To set timings:
   CLICK: [▷] after the clock reaches 5 seconds
   CLICK: [▷] every 5 seconds, for each remaining slide

4. When the slide show is finished, PowerPoint displays a dialog box showing the total number of seconds that have elapsed. To record the timings:
   CLICK: Yes command button

5. To review the timings in Slide Sorter view:
   CLICK: Yes command button

6. To view the presentation with the new timings:
   CLICK: Slide Show view button (▣)
   Now, sit back and watch the show! (*Hint:* You can also choose Slide Show, Set Up Show from the Menu bar and then select the *Loop continuously until 'Esc'* check box for self-running displays at trade shows and other presentations.)

7. Save the "INFS 101" presentation to your Data Files location.

QUICK REFERENCE
Setting Timings

1. **CHOOSE: Slide Show, Rehearse Timings**
2. **CLICK: the mouse button after the desired seconds on each slide**
3. **After viewing the entire presentation:**
   CLICK: Yes command button to record the slide timings
   CLICK: Yes command button to review the timings

IN ADDITION PLAYING MULTIPLE PRESENTATIONS CONSECUTIVELY

With PowerPoint, you can run multiple presentations consecutively, even unattended. When the first presentation is finished, the second presentation automatically begins. To do this, you assemble a *play list*.

For more information on this topic, choose Help, Contents and Index and then click the *Index* tab. Type **play lists** and then click the Display button to display a list of related topics.

ADDING TRANSITIONS

In this section, you learn to incorporate transitions between slides. Transitions are the special effects you see when you go from one slide to the next. Previously only available in higher-end multimedia authoring programs, transitions can now be easily inserted into any of your PowerPoint presentations.

Now you will add transitions to the "INFS 101" presentation.

Perform the following steps . . .

1. Display "INFS 101" presentation in Slide Sorter view. (*Note:* Ensure that slides 1–6 appear.)

2. To add a transition to slide 1:
SELECT: slide 1
CLICK: Transition button (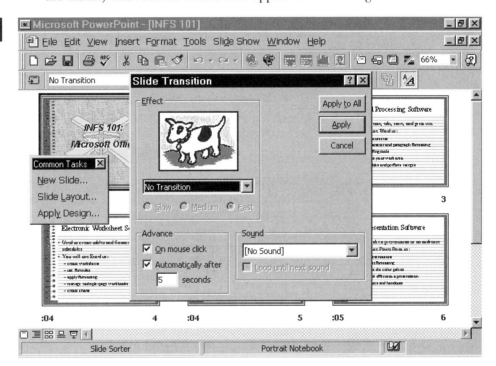) on the Slide Sorter toolbar
(*Note:* You can also choose the Slide Show, Slide Transition command from the menu.) Your screen should now appear similar to Figure 4.10.

FIGURE 4.10

TRANSITION DIALOG BOX

3. CLICK: down arrow beside the *Effect* drop-down list box
(*Note:* You can also display the same options by selecting the *Transition Effects* drop-down list box in the Slide Sorter toolbar.)

4. CLICK: several transition effects
Notice that they appear in the preview area of the dialog box.

5. SELECT: Checkerboard Across

6. PRESS: [ENTER] or CLICK: Apply
When you run the slide show, slide 1 will display with the Checkerboard Across transition.

7. SELECT: slide 2
SELECT: Blinds Vertical from the *Slide Transition Effects* drop-down list box in the Slide Sorter toolbar

8. For each of the remaining slides:
SELECT: a different transition effect from the *Slide Transition Effects* drop-down list

9. To view the slide show:
CLICK: Slide Show view button ()
CLICK: the left mouse button until you've seen the entire show

10. When the presentation is finished, the presentation will again display in Slide Sorter view. (*Note:* In this view mode, you can see how a particular slide will transition by clicking the transition icon that is located on the bottom-left of each slide. Also, if timing is present, it appears below its image.)

QUICK REFERENCE
Applying Transitions

1. **CLICK: Slide Sorter view button ()**
2. **SELECT: any slide in the presentation**
3. **CLICK: Transition button () on the Slide Sorter toolbar**
4. **SELECT: a transition effect**
5. **PRESS: ENTER or CLICK: OK**

CREATING A BUILD SLIDE

Build slides let you reveal one bullet at a time in Slide Show view. You can also specify how the bullet appears (e.g., enters from the right), and whether you want to dim previously displayed items when you display a new bulleted item.

Next you create a build slide.

Perform the following steps . . .

1. Ensure that the "INFS 101" presentation appears in Slide Sorter view.

2. To add a build slide to the presentation:
SELECT: slide 4 in Slide Sorter view
(*Note:* This slide contains bulleted items describing electronic worksheet software.)

3. To create a build slide:
CLICK: down arrow beside the *Text Preset Animation* drop-down list box on the Slide Sorter toolbar
(*Note:* You can also choose the Slide Show, Preset Animation command from the menu.)

4. SELECT: Fly From Top

5. To display slide 4 in Slide Show view:
CLICK: Slide Show view button ()
The bullets appear one by one on the slide. If no timings were built into this presentation, you would need to click to display each bullet.

6. On your own, experiment with adding build effects to the remaining slides in the presentation.

7. Save the "INFS 101" presentation to your Data Files location.

QUICK REFERENCE
Creating a Build Slide

1. **CLICK: Slide Sorter view button (88)**
2. **SELECT: any slide in the presentation**
3. **CLICK: down arrow beside the *Text Preset Animation* drop-down list box on the Slide Sorter toolbar**
4. **SELECT: a build effect**

ADDING ANIMATION

Does your computer have a sound card and speakers? If so, you can play sound effects and add animation to your presentations. For example, you can listen to screeching brakes as text rolls in from the left side of the screen; how about hearing a laser sound as each letter drops into place or a whoosh sound as text races in from the left. These animated effects combine sound and motion and are only a few of the effects accessible from the Animation Effects toolbar. By adding a bit of drama to your presentation, these effects will not only keep your audience interested but also entertained. The Animation Effects toolbar appears below.

In this section, you use the Animation Effects toolbar to animate a slide in the "INFS 101" presentation.

Perform the following steps . . .

1. Ensure that slide 4 of the "INFS 101" presentation appears in Slide view.

2. To display the Animation Effects toolbar:
   CLICK: Animation Effects button ( ) on the Standard toolbar

3. If the Animation Effects toolbar is covering part of your slide, drag it to one of the edges of the presentation window.

4. Notice that many of the buttons on the Animation Effects toolbar aren't available. This is because you must first select the object you want to animate. To select the Text placeholder:
   CLICK: in the Text placeholder (containing the bulleted items)
   Your screen should now appear similar to Figure 4.11.

FIGURE 4.11

THE ANIMATION
EFFECTS TOOLBAR

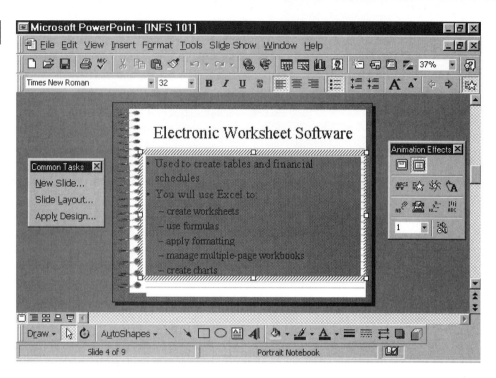

5. In this step, you are going to add the Laser Text Effect (🔲) to the bulleted text on slide 4.
CLICK: Laser Text Effect button (🔲)

6. To see the effect of the animation:
CLICK: Slide Show view button (🖳)
The bulleted text should be "flying" into place.

7. PRESS: ESC to display the presentation in Slide view

8. On your own, try out other animation effects.

9. Before proceeding, remove the Animation Effects toolbar from view.
CLICK: Animation Effects button (🌠) on the Standard toolbar

10. Save "INFS 101" to your Data Files location.

QUICK REFERENCE
Adding Animation Effects

1. **CLICK: Animation Effects button (🌠) on the Standard toolbar**
2. **CLICK: the area of the slide you want to animate**
3. **CLICK: the desired effect on the Animation Effects toolbar**

CREATING A CUSTOM SLIDE SHOW

With PowerPoint, you can customize a slide show to meet your specific needs. For example, in its current form, the "INFS 101" presentation is suited to an audience of students that is already enrolled in the INFS 101 course. It contains very specific information about the course. But what if you want to show the same slide show to an audience of prospective students? You would probably want to reduce the level of detail, eliminating slides that get too specific.

Using the Slide Show, Custom Show command, you can easily customize a slide show to your needs. You simply select the slides you want to include in the custom show and decide how you want them ordered. The major advantage of this feature is that you don't need to store multiple copies of the same presentation on disk.

Now you practice creating a custom show from the "INFS 101" presentation.

Perform the following steps . . .

1. Display the "INFS 101" presentation in Slide view.

2. CHOOSE: Slide Show, Custom Show from the Menu bar
The Custom Show dialog box appears.

3. To create a new custom show:
CLICK: New command button
The dialog box in Figure 4.12 appears.

FIGURE 4.12

CREATING A CUSTOM SHOW

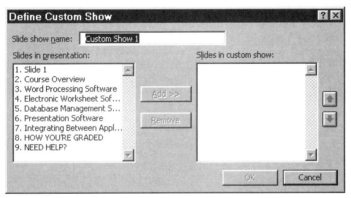

4. Let's type in a name for the custom show. The default name is *Custom Show #*.
TYPE: **Prospective Students**

5. You will now add slides 1–7 in the custom show, excluding slides 8–9 because they contain information that is too specific for the intended audience.
CLICK: the first slide in the *Slides in presentation* list box
CLICK: Add command button
Slide 1 was added to the *Slides in custom show* list box.

6. To add a group of slides, you hold down CTRL and click the slides in the *Slides in presentation* box that you want to select.
PRESS: CTRL and hold it down
CLICK: slides 2–7 in the *Slides in presentation* list box

7. Release the CTRL key.

8. To add the selected slides to the custom show:
CLICK: Add command button
The Define Custom Show dialog box should now appear similar to Figure 4.13.

FIGURE 4.13

DEFINING THE
CUSTOM SHOW

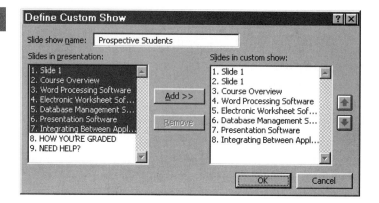

9. To proceed:
PRESS: **ENTER** or CLICK: OK
The Custom Show dialog box appears.

10. To view the show, click the Show button.
CLICK: Show command button
The slide show will run in a continuous loop.

11. To exit Slide Show view:
PRESS: **ESC**
In the future, when you want to view the custom show, you choose Slide Show, Custom Show and select the custom show you want to view. Then click the Show command button.

12. To remove the Custom Shows dialog box:
CLICK: Close

13. Save "INFS 101" to your Data Files location.

14. Exit Microsoft PowerPoint.

QUICK REFERENCE
Creating a Custom
Slide Show

1. **CHOOSE: Slide Show, Custom Shows**

2. **CLICK: New button to create a new custom show**

3. **SELECT: the slides in the *Slides in presentation* list box**

4. **CLICK: Add command button**

5. **PRESS: ENTER or CLICK: OK**

IN ADDITION LINKING YOUR PRESENTATION TO THE INTERNET AND OTHER MICROSOFT
OFFICE DOCUMENTS

You can create links in your presentation to Internet addresses or to other Microsoft Office documents on your hard drive or network drive. When you click the link, you move to the desired location. These links are called *hyperlinks*. To include hyperlinks in your presentation, you click the Insert Hyperlink button (🦆) on the

Standard toolbar and then answer the questions in the Insert Hyperlink dialog box.

For more information, choose Help, Contents and Index. Click the *Contents* tab and select the "Working with Presentations on Intranets and the Internet" topic. Then explore the "Working with Hyperlinks" topic.

Summary

This session focused on adding visual objects and effects to your presentations. You learned about editing clip art using the Picture toolbar. You also learned to insert a graph and an organization chart on a slide using Microsoft Graph and Microsoft Organization Chart. Next you added some special effects to an electronic presentation. Specifically, you added timing and transitions, created build slides, and added animated effects. The session concluded by showing you how to create a custom slide show.

COMMAND SUMMARY

Many of the commands and procedures appearing in this session are provided in Table 4.1 below.

TABLE 4.1	*Task Description*	*Menu Command*	*Alternative Method*
Command Summary	Insert a clip art image	Insert, Picture, Clip Art	🖼
	Insert a graph	Insert, Chart	📊
	Insert an organization chart	Insert, Picture, Organization Chart	
	Build timings into a slide show	Slide Show, Rehearse Timings	
	Add transitions to a slide show (from Slide Sorter view)	Slide Show, Slide Transition	🖥
	Create build slides (from Slide Sorter view)	Slide Show, Preset Animation	
	Add animated effects		⭐

KEY TERMS

graphic file

A computer graphic, created by an artist or scanned from an existing picture or photograph, that you can insert into your document using the Insert, Picture command.

Microsoft Graph

A supplementary program or *mini-app* that lets you create graphs and insert them onto a PowerPoint slide.

Microsoft Organization Chart

A supplementary program or *mini-app* that lets you create organization charts and insert them onto a PowerPoint slide.

mini-apps

Small application programs that are bundled with Microsoft Windows products to enhance the primary applications; most mini-apps are accessed using the Insert, Object command.

organization charts

A diagram showing the internal management reporting structure of a company, organization, institution, or other such group; also used for flowchart diagrams.

scanner

A hardware device that converts an existing picture or photograph into a computer image that is stored digitally on the disk.

EXERCISES

SHORT ANSWER

1. How would you brighten a clip art image?

2. What is a custom show? Provide an example of when you might want to create a custom show.

3. What is the difference between inserting a clip art image using the Clip Art button on the Standard toolbar and using a Clip Art autolayout?

4. Describe some of the effects accessible using the Animation Effects toolbar.

5. What is the procedure for editing a graph object once it has been inserted on a slide?

6. Why would you want to build timing into a presentation?

7. Describe two methods for inserting an organization chart object on a slide.

8. In an electronic slide show, what is a transition? Give some examples.

9. Describe the process of creating and inserting a graph on a slide.

10. What is a build slide? Give some examples of build effects.

HANDS-ON

(*Note:* Ensure that you know the location of your Advantage Files and where to store your Data Files. If necessary, ask your instructor or lab assistant for additional information.)

1. Open the "Melon" presentation that is stored in the Advantage Files location. Perform the following modifications to the presentation:

   a. Make slides 2–4 build slides.

   b. Specify timings and transitions between all the slides in the presentation.

   c. Create a custom show called "December Trade Show" that includes slides 1 and 2.

   d. Save the presentation as "R.C. Melon" to your Data Files location.

2. Create a presentation that includes the five slides pictured in Figure 4.14. Create build slides, and add transitions and timings. Then, save the presentation as "PC Hardware Components" to your Data Files location.

FIGURE 4.14

SLIDE 1

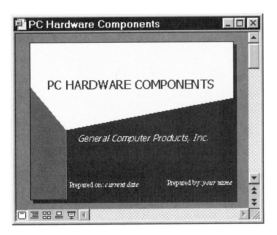

SLIDE 2

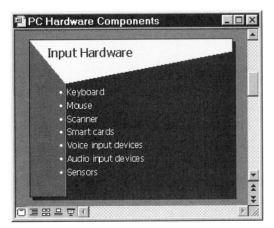

SLIDE 3

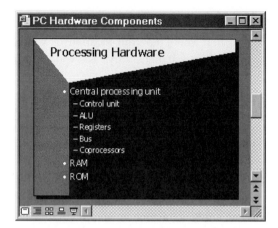

SLIDE 4

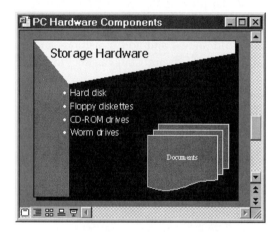

SLIDE 5

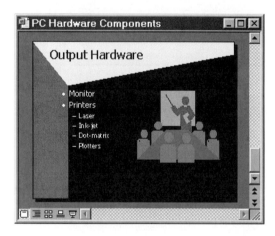

3. On your own, create a slide show describing a fictitious company, such as *Wally's Widgets*. The presentation should include six slides that contain the information listed below. When you're finished, save the presentation as "On Your Own-5" to your Data Files location.

   a. Company name, address, and phone information (include a clip art image)

   b. Description of the product (features and benefits)

   c. Pricing information

   d. Projected sales (include a graph)

   e. Personnel (include an organization chart)

   f. Summary slide

4. On your own, create an electronic presentation using PowerPoint's "Generic (Standard)" presentation template. You access this template in the *Presentations* tab of the New Presentation dialog box. Adapt this presentation to a topic you're interested in. When finished, save the presentation as "On Your Own-6" to your Data Files location. The presentation should contain at least five slides and include the following:

   a. A clip art image

   b. An autoshape image

   c. Text that you've inserted with the Text tool

   d. Customized bullets

   e. Build slides

   f. Timings and transitions between slides

   g. Animated effects

CASE PROBLEMS | **IMMACULATE PERCEPTIONS, INC. (IPI)**

(*Note:* In the following case problems, assume the role of the primary character or characters and perform the same steps that they identify.)

1. It was late Friday afternoon and most of the staff had already left the IPI offices for the long weekend. Roy MacGregor, on the other hand, was just arriving at IPI for the first time that day. Roy is the marketing manager for IPI and had taken an early commuter flight to Portland that morning to spend the day with a new client. Both Connie and Bobbie went to their office doors to greet him, but Roy got the first words out. "You're never going to believe this! I just spent an entire day with Gloria Gallego at Windermere's Windshield Wiper Warehouse. We had a $400,000 contract tied up by lunch and then she asked me some ridiculous questions about

presentation software." Connie and Bobbie stole a quick glance at each other as Roy proceeded with his story. "Four hundred big ones down the drain because we can't deliver some sort of electronic slide show for their trade show exhibit. I've never even heard of the thing before—something like PowerPress or Point-to-Power, I don't know!"

Connie and Bobbie led Roy to the boardroom and explained the meeting they had held with the creative staff that morning. Connie added, "We can do this presentation for them, Roy. I want you to call Gloria immediately and tell her that we'll send a sample presentation by Tuesday afternoon. Did you take any notes of what they wanted in an electronic slide show?" After shuffling some papers back and forth, Roy handed Connie one page of notes and left for his office to call Gloria.

Upon Roy's return, Connie had summarized what the presentation should look like and what information it should contain. Using the following notes, you must now create a presentation for Windermere's Windshield Wiper Warehouse.

PowerPoint Presentation for Windermere's Windshield Wiper Warehouse

The presentation must include the following features:

- *Be continuously self-running for display in trade show booths*

- *Use their corporate colors of White, Black, and Red*

- *Use transitions that wipe left and right like windshield wipers*

- *Contain transportation-related clip art, like the image of a car*

- *Contain 8 slides with the following content*

#1: An introduction slide with the company's name and the clip art image of a car	#2: Why W4 Wipers Work Best ● Lifetime rubber compound ● Durable steel construction ● Tested and guaranteed
#3: Lifetime Rubber Compound ● Lasts forever and a day ● New coating stops streaking ● Good from −30 to over 100 degrees in temperature	#4: Durable Steel Construction ● Lasts forever and a day ● Maintenance-free parts ● Carried by hundreds of mechanics on the West Coast
#5: Tested and Guaranteed ● Used on many makes and models of automobiles ● Certified by the Windshield Manufacturer's Association	#6: Company name again ● Friendly, courteous staff ● Toll-free phone number ● Terms of credit available (make this a build slide)
#7: A summary slide of the major points. Make it the same as slide #2 to save time.	#8: A conclusion slide with the company name and a message that the presentation will begin again in 15 seconds.

After viewing the presentation in Slide Show view, save the file as "Windermere" to your Data Files location.

2. Connie and Bobbie have been asked to present a company overview to the board of directors of IPI. This is a very formal presentation to their lawyers, accountants, bankers, and major investors. Create a PowerPoint presentation with an introduction and conclusion slide, and include the following components. Save the presentation as "IPI Board" to your Data Files location.

Company Products

- *Image consulting*
- *Trade show materials*
- *Point-of-purchase displays*
- *PowerPoint presentations*

Growth History (1991 to 1996)

- *Staff: 2 to 14*
- *Clients: 8 to 26*
- *Sales: $65,000 to $1.6 million*

Staff

- *Two directors*
- *Two managers*
- *Six creative staff*
- *Four administrative personnel*

Organization Chart

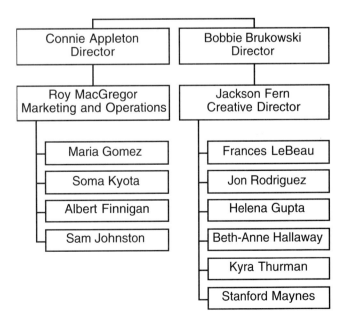

3. Add the following financial projections to the "IPI Board" presentation, complete with a table of figures on one slide and a graph on another. Also, incorporate slide transition effects and use build slides in the presentation. Save the presentation back to your Data Files location.

(in 000s)	*1995*	*1996*
Sales Revenue	$1,450	$1,620
Cost of Sales	580	700
Gross Profit	870	920
Fixed Costs	450	480
Net Profit	$420	$440

Microsoft PowerPoint 97 for Windows

Notes, Handouts, and Printing

SESSION

5

IRWIN

COMPUTER & INFORMATION TECHNOLOGY

INTRODUCTION

In this session, you learn to create and print speakers notes and audience handouts, two useful components of any presentation. Like slides, notes and handouts have associated masters called the Notes Master and the Handout Master, respectively. You also learn to print the different elements of your presentation, including how to set up a 35 mm slide format for output.

SPRINGS COLLEGE, COLORADO

Situated on a hillside of fir trees with a breathtaking view of the valley, the Springs College campus provides a beautiful and convenient retreat for residents of Denver and Colorado Springs. In addition to its surroundings, the school is well known in the state for its progressive business and computer programs. Bradley Neumann was very fortunate to land his first-ever teaching position with Springs College, especially considering his alternative offer from Wolf Bay University in Canada's Northwest Territories!

After two months, Bradley felt comfortable with the marketing courses that he had recently assumed from Gayle Fanning, who was taking a year's sabbatical to conduct marketing research for a large computer manufacturer. He wasn't expecting to hear from Gayle for another ten months when he received an e-mail over the Internet: *Hi Bradley, I trust that you're into the full swing of things now that it's been a couple of months. I've been collecting some very interesting research that I think you should include in your Marketing Research 201 curriculum. I've received authorization from the company I'm working with to send you reports every two weeks with my findings and conclusions. I think this information will greatly benefit your students. I'll be in touch soon, Gayle.*

In this session, you and Bradley will learn to create speaker's notes pages and audience handouts. These two elements of a presentation are extremely valuable when you are presenting someone else's ideas and need the supporting documentation close at hand. You also learn to create 35 mm slides for taking your presentations on the road.

PUBLIC SPEAKING TIPS

One of the greatest skills that you can possess is a talent for public speaking. Whatever career choice you've made or will make, the time will come when you must present an opinion, train a co-worker, or give an impromptu speech at your son's or daughter's kindergarten class. In the real world, however, some people would rather streak across the field during the Super Bowl than say a few words in front of their peers.

Here are some techniques to help you combat your platform jitters and pull off a winning presentation:

- Prepare your presentation materials thoroughly.
- Practice your delivery in front of the mirror or using a tape recorder.
- Polish your delivery (e.g., remember to make eye contact).
- Psyche yourself up and project positive thoughts.
- Visualize yourself doing an excellent job!

When preparing to give a presentation, allot yourself approximately two minutes to present each slide. Therefore, a 30-minute presentation will have about 15 slides. You may feel that you need more content than this to "save you" for half an hour, but the actual time that it takes to present a slide to an audience is rarely less than two minutes. You do not want to put all your information into your slide presentation anyway. Otherwise, you might as well just distribute handouts to the audience and send them on their way. Remember, the audience is there to listen to what you will say and how you will say it! Every successful speaker communicates his or her interest and enthusiasm in a topic and remains courteous to the audience at all times.

SPEAKER'S NOTES

In preparing for a presentation, you should consider creating cheat sheets or crib notes. These notes help you avoid a common pitfall among novice presenters—putting too much text on the slides. Keep your slides brief and to the point. Use the notes pages in PowerPoint (as a replacement or complement to your recipe cards) to store reminders to yourself, relevant facts, and anecdotes. These notes pages also come in handy for question periods at the end of presentations.

In PowerPoint, a typical **notes page** provides a smaller, printed version of a slide at the top of the page with an area for text and graphics appearing below. Using the Notes Master, you can add designs and logos to all of your notes pages, or you can edit individual pages. To select the Notes Page view, click the Notes Page view button (⊟) or choose View, Notes Page from the menu.

CREATING AND PRINTING SPEAKER'S NOTES

In this section, you create a notes page for the "Training" presentation that is stored in your Advantage Files location.

Perform the following steps . . .

1. Open the "Training" presentation from the Advantage Files location.

2. The first slide of the "Training" presentation should appear in the presentation window.

3. CLICK: Notes Page view button (⊟)
   SELECT: 50% from the *Zoom* drop-down list box
   Your screen should now appear similar to Figure 5.1.

FIGURE 5.1

A NOTES PAGE FROM
THE "TRAINING"
PRESENTATION

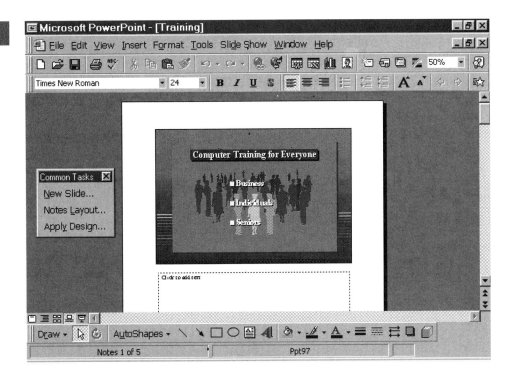

4. To add notes:
   CLICK: anywhere in the notes box to position the insertion point

5. To enlarge your view of the notes box so it's easier to see:
   SELECT: 75% from the *Zoom* drop-down list box
   (*Hint:* As needed, you can also resize the page space taken up by the
   image or notes area by selecting the area's border and dragging its handles.)

6. Ensure that the insertion point or cursor is blinking inside the notes box.
   Do the following:
   TYPE: Welcome to MPC College.
   PRESS: (ENTER) twice
   TYPE: And welcome to our first computer training ori-
   entation meeting. We are anxious to share with you
   the elements of our training program and to take you
   on a tour of MPC's training facilities.
   PRESS: (ENTER) twice
   TYPE: Please feel free to ask questions at any point
   during the presentation.

   Your screen should now appear similar to Figure 5.2.

FIGURE 5.2

ENTERING TEXT INTO
A NOTES PAGE

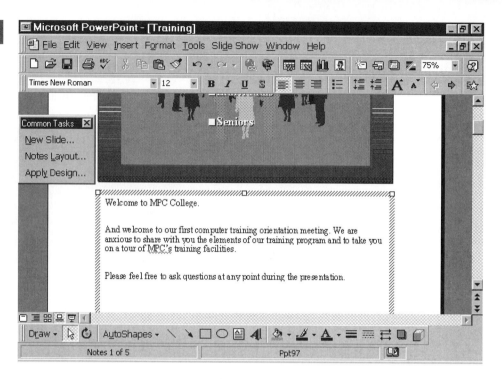

7. To print the notes page:
CHOOSE: File, Print
CLICK: down arrow beside the *Print what* drop-down list box
SELECT: Notes Pages

8. To print just the current slide:
SELECT: Current Slide option button in the *Print range* area
PRESS: (**ENTER**) or CLICK: OK

QUICK REFERENCE
Creating a Notes Page

1. **Make the desired slide active in the presentation window.**

2. **CHOOSE: View, Notes Page, or**
CLICK: Notes Page view button (🖳)

3. **CLICK: anywhere in the Notes placeholder box**

4. **TYPE:** *desired notes*

MODIFYING THE NOTES MASTER

Let's place your name in the footer of the Notes Master. A *footer* is a word processing term for the area that appears at the bottom of every page. A *header* is a
word processing term for the area that appears at the top of every page. This page
currently has a footer with the page number and current slide number. You can
also insert clip art images and other graphic pictures in the header and footer of
a page.

**Perform
the
following
steps . . .**

1. To create a footer that appears on every page, you need to modify the Notes Master. Let's display this master page:
CHOOSE: View, Master, Notes Master
(*Note:* You can also press **SHIFT** and then click the Notes Page view button (⬛) to display the Notes Master.)

2. DRAG: the elevator scroll box to the bottom of the vertical scroll bar so that you can see the bottom of the page

3. Click the mouse button in the bottom left-hand corner of the page in the Footer Area text box. The text box is selected.

4. To change the point size of the text:
CLICK: down arrow beside the *Font Size* drop-down list box
SELECT: 12

5. TYPE: **Presented by** *your name*
Enter your name where specified in the above instruction. Your screen should now appear similar to Figure 5.3. (*Note:* The <footer> placeholder is non-printing and will not appear in your printout.)

FIGURE 5.3

THE MODIFIED NOTES
MASTER

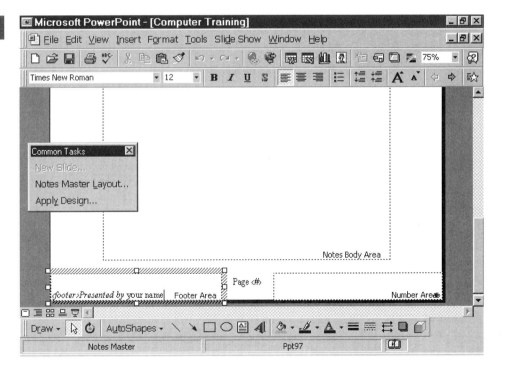

6. To return to the Notes Pages view:
CLICK: Notes Page view button (⬛)
Notice that the text you entered above now appears in the footer of the active page. Also, the current page number appears centered and the current slide number appears in the bottom-right corner.

7. Save your work as "Computer Training" to your Data Files location.

QUICK REFERENCE
Modifying the Notes
Master

1. **CHOOSE: View, Master, Notes Master**
2. **Modify the formatting specifications of the Text placeholder or add text and graphics to the Notes Master.**

IN ADDITION INSERTING COMMENTS

When a presentation is produced as part of a collaborative effort, a handy feature is to be able to insert comments directly into the presentation. To do this in PowerPoint:

1. Display the Reviewing toolbar.
2. Display the appropriate slide.

3. CLICK: Insert Comment button ([⬚]) on the Reviewing toolbar
4. TYPE: a comment into the text box

If you don't want comments to appear in the presentation, click the Show/Hide Comments button ([⬚]) on the Reviewing toolbar.

AUDIENCE HANDOUTS

Preparing handouts for your audience is a courtesy. However, you do not want to provide too much information in audience handouts; otherwise, there is no incentive to sit through your presentation. Many presenters create audience handouts in which important information is missing from the slide representations on the page. As the speaker proceeds through each slide, important information is provided so that the audience can fill in the blanks in their notes. Not only does the audience have to pay attention in order to compile a complete set of notes, they may also remember the important concepts better by having to write them down.

In PowerPoint, a handout is essentially a printout of the slides in your presentation. As with the notes pages, you can add text and art—such as your company logo—to all of the handout pages. You also choose whether to include two, three, or six slides on a handout page. Another option to consider is leaving space on the handout so that your audience can take notes during the presentation. In the following sections, you create a handout for the "Computer Training" presentation that is stored in your Data Files location.

MODIFYING THE HANDOUT MASTER

You add text and graphics to a handout by modifying the Handout Master. Unlike notes pages, handouts cannot be edited individually. In fact, you see them only after they are printed.

Perform the following steps . . .

1. Ensure that the first slide of the "Computer Training" presentation appears in the presentation window.

2. CHOOSE: View, Master, Handout Master
   Your screen should now look similar to Figure 5.4.

FIGURE 5.4

HANDOUT MASTER WITH OUTLINES SHOWING WHERE TWO, THREE, AND SIX SLIDES WILL PRINT

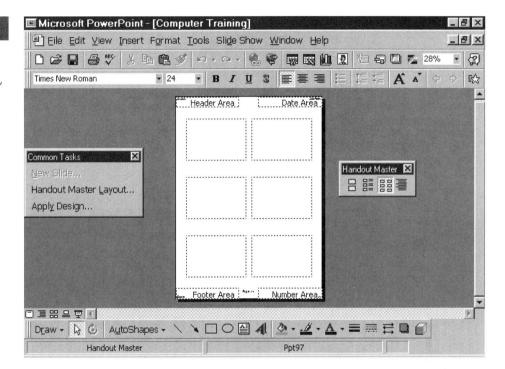

3. To enlarge your view of the handout page:
   CLICK: down arrow beside the *Zoom* drop-down list
   SELECT: 75%

4. DRAG: the elevator scroll box to the top of the vertical scroll bar

5. In this step, you insert a title in the header. Do the following:
   CLICK: the mouse pointer in the upper left-hand corner of the page (in the Header Area text box)

6. To change the point size of the text:
   CLICK: down arrow beside the *Font Size* drop-down list box
   SELECT: 18

7. TYPE: MPC College:
   PRESS: (ENTER)
   TYPE: Computer Training Center
   Your screen should now appear similar to Figure 5.5.

FIGURE 5.5

TEXT INSERTED IN THE
HEADER OF THE
HANDOUT MASTER

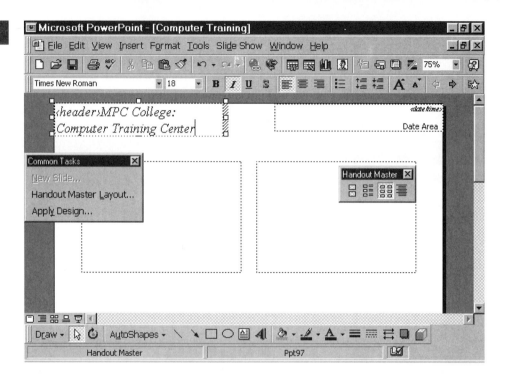

8. Display the presentation in Slide view.

QUICK REFERENCE
Modifying the
Handout Master

1. **CHOOSE: View, Master, Handout Master**
2. **Modify the formatting specifications of the Text placeholder or add text and graphics to the Handout Master.**

PRINTING AUDIENCE HANDOUTS

To print audience handouts for the "Computer Training" presentation, perform the following steps.

Perform the following steps . . .

1. CHOOSE: File, Print
   CLICK: down arrow beside the *Print what* drop-down list box
   SELECT: Handouts (6 slides per page)

2. To print the entire presentation:
   SELECT: All option button in the *Print range* area
   PRESS: (ENTER) or CLICK: OK

3. To prepare for the next section:
   CLICK: Slide view button
   CHOOSE: Fit from the *Zoom* drop-down list box

QUICK REFERENCE	1. **CHOOSE:** File, Print
Printing Audience Handout Pages	2. **SELECT:** Handouts (number of slides per page) from the *Print what* drop-down list box
	3. **SELECT:** the desired handouts to print in the *Print range* area
	4. **PRESS:** ⟨ENTER⟩ or **CLICK:** OK

PRINT OPTIONS FOR SLIDES

As you've seen throughout this learning guide, the process of printing involves first opening the presentation you want to print, identifying what you want to print (slides, outline, notes pages, audience handouts) and then specifying the range of slides to print.

In the following sections, we describe some additional options that you should be familiar with when printing your presentations.

SETTING UP THE SLIDE FORMAT

The size of your printed slides is determined by the settings in the Page Setup box (Figure 5.6). If you don't want to use the default settings, you should choose File, Page Setup to establish the settings *before* you begin creating slides. Review the options in Table 5.1 for more information. **Landscape orientation** means that what you print will print across the length of the paper. In **portrait orientation**, a slide image would appear taller than in landscape orientation.

TABLE 5.1	*Slide Output*	*Width*	*Height*	*Orientation*
Slide Dimensions	On-Screen Show	10 inches	7.5 inches	Landscape
	Letter Paper (8.5 × 11 inches)	10 inches	7.5 inches	Landscape
	A4 Paper (210 mm × 297 mm)	10.83 inches	7.5 inches	Landscape
	35 mm slide	11.25 inches	7.5 inches	Landscape
	Overhead	10 inches	7.5 inches	Landscape
	Custom (your own settings)			

Perform the following steps . . .

1. Ensure that the first slide of the "Computer Training" presentation appears in the presentation window.

2. To display the Slide Setup dialog box:
CHOOSE: File, Page Setup
The Page Setup dialog box appears (Figure 5.6).

FIGURE 5.6

PAGE SETUP DIALOG BOX

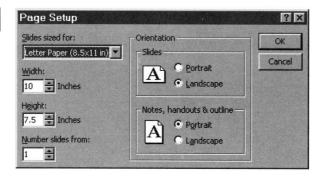

3. CLICK: down arrow beside the *Slides Sized for* drop-down list box

4. Review the options in the drop-down list box and do the following:
SELECT: Cancel command button to leave the dialog box

5. Save the "Computer Training" presentation to your Data Files location.

6. Close the presentation and exit Microsoft PowerPoint.

35 MM SLIDES

If you will be creating 35 mm slides of your presentation, make sure to first select 35 mm slides in the Page Setup dialog box (described in the previous section). Then you choose File, Print to display the Print dialog box. Select the *Scale to Fit Paper* check box to have PowerPoint scale your slides so that they will fit. Select the *Print to File* check box in order to create a file that can be turned over to an outside service bureau for the creation of 35 mm slides. (*Note:* After you press (ENTER), PowerPoint prompts you for the name of the slide file.)

For more convenience, if you are in North America and have a modem in your computer, you can send your presentation directly from PowerPoint to Genigraphics, a company that specializes in the output of color 35 mm slides and other types of color output. Choose the File, Send to Genigraphics command from the Menu bar and then follow the instructions presented by the Genigraphics wizard. (*Note:* If the "Send to Genigraphics" option doesn't appear in the File menu, then this option wasn't installed on your computer.)

<table>
<tr><td colspan="2">

QUICK REFERENCE
Creating 35 mm Slides

</td><td>

1. **CHOOSE: File, Page Setup**
   SELECT: 35 mm slides in the *Slides Sized for* drop-down list box
   PRESS: [ENTER] or CLICK: OK
2. **CHOOSE: File, Print**
   SELECT: Slides in the *Print what* drop-down list box
   SELECT: *Print to File* check box
   SELECT: *Scale to Fit Paper* check box
   PRESS: [ENTER] or CLICK: OK
3. **PowerPoint will prompt you for the name of the output file.**

</td></tr>
</table>

Packaging your presentation

If you typically present PowerPoint presentations on different computers, you need to know about the Pack And Go Wizard. This helpful wizard packages your entire presentation, including the PowerPoint Viewer program (if desired), into a single file. In fact, you can even package multiple presentations together on the same diskette or across several diskettes. For an added sense of security and to ensure that the presentation looks the same on another computer, the Pack And Go Wizard lets you include linked files and embed TrueType fonts. Lastly, the wizard compresses the presentation so that it takes a lesser number of diskettes to take your show on the road! For more information on this topic, refer to the PowerPoint online Help facility or run the command by choosing File, Pack And Go.

IN ADDITION EXPORTING YOUR SLIDES AND NOTES PAGES TO A WORD DOCUMENT

1. CHOOSE: File, Send To
2. CHOOSE: Microsoft Word
3. SELECT: *Notes next to slides* or *Notes below slides* option button

4. PRESS: [ENTER] or CLICK: OK

Summary

In this session, you learned how to create and print notes pages and audience handouts. You used the Notes Master and the Handout Master to include text or other objects in the headers and footers of every notes or handout page. The session concluded by showing you how to use the Page Setup dialog box and how to print 35 mm slides.

COMMAND SUMMARY

Many of the commands and procedures appearing in this session are provided in Table 5.2 below.

TABLE 5.2

Command Summary

Task Description	Menu Command
Display the Notes Master	View, Master, Notes Master
Display the Handout Master	View, Master, Handout Master
Display the Page Setup dialog box	File, Page Setup
Print 35 mm slides	File, Print
Package a presentation for delivery on another computer	File, Pack And Go

KEY TERMS

landscape orientation
In this mode, your slides print across the length of the page.

notes page
A notes page, used by the presenter, that includes a smaller printed version of a slide on the top of the page and an area for notes below.

portrait orientation
In this mode, your slides print across the width of the page.

EXERCISES

SHORT ANSWER

1. When might you need to use the Page Setup dialog box?
2. When might you want to modify the Notes Master?
3. What are the dotted lines that appear on the Handout Master?
4. What is the *Zoom* drop-down list box used for?
5. How do you change the orientation of the slides you print?
6. What does the Pack And Go Wizard do?
7. If you want all your notes pages to print with a larger notes area and a smaller screen image, what should you do?
8. How do you create 35 mm slides?
9. What does a notes page look like? What does a handout look like?
10. How do you include text on an audience handout?

HANDS-ON

(*Note:* Ensure that you know the location of your Advantage Files and where to store your Data Files. If necessary, ask your instructor or lab assistant for additional information.)

1. Open the "Travel" presentation that is stored in the Advantage Files location. This presentation contains a few slides from a more in-depth presentation. Perform the following steps.

   a. Display slide 1 in Notes Page view.

   b. Type in a few sentences of notes that would be helpful when presenting this slide.

   c. Create notes for slides 2 and 3 also.

   d. Print the notes pages.

   e. Display the Handout Master.

   f. Type the current date in the upper right-hand corner of each page and your name in the bottom-left corner of each page.

   g. Print the handouts.

   h. Save the presentation as "Travel Today" to your Data Files location.

   i. Close the presentation.

2. Open "Palette," a two-slide presentation, from the Advantage Files location. This presentation is intended to run in a continuous loop at a Home Improvements trade show. Embellish the presentation with the features we list below. Then save the presentation to your Data Files location as "The Master Palette."

   a. Apply a design to the presentation.

   b. Insert an autoshape on slide 1 that captures the viewer's attention.

   c. Add a clip art image to slide 2.

   d. Make slide 2 a build slide and add transition effects to both slides.

   e. In order to be prepared in case you're asked questions, create a Notes Page for each page for both slides, containing data you can refer to.

   f. Print the notes pages for your reference during the trade show.

3. On your own, use what you've learned in this learning guide to create an informative presentation about a topic of your choice or one given to you by your instructor. Your presentation should be organized with a clear objective and should contain at least 5 slides. Try to make your presentation as visually captivating as possible. When you're finished, save the presentation as "On Your Own-7" to your Data Files location.

SPRINGS COLLEGE, COLORADO

(*Note:* In the following case problems, assume the role of the primary character or characters and perform the same steps that they identify.)

1. Ten days pass before Bradley receives an e-mail from Gayle (shown below). After perusing the information, he determines that the content fits nicely with an upcoming lecture he is giving on the general steps involved in conducting market research. After printing the message, Bradley highlights the points that he wants to include on the slides. The remaining information will have to go into his speaker's notes. He proceeds to create a presentation consisting of seven slides: five content slides, an introduction slide, and a summary slide. After adding some clip art images, transitions, and build slides to the presentation, he saves his work as "Marketing" to his Data Files location. As the final step, Bradley prints the slides, speaker's notes pages, and audience handouts.

Date: Nov. 15, 1996
To: Bradley Neumann
From: Gayle Fanning
Subject: Steps in Marketing Research
cc:

A marketing research project involves the following steps:

1. ***Specify Your Objectives***
   *As a marketing researcher, you must know the **reasons for conducting the research**. Also, you must **properly define the process** to ensure that you will gather information on which you can base decisions. Don't let managers request unnecessary research based on their own excitement.*

2. ***Determine the Data Sources***
   *You must determine whether the information can and should be gathered from **internal sources** or from **external sources**. Internal sources are a company's financial statements and management information system reports. External sources include newspapers, trade journals, and government or industry reports.*

3. ***Define the Sample***
   *To provide information of any use, you must find a representative population sample. Issues that you must take into consideration include the **size of the sample** and the **data collection methods** you will use.*

4. ***Collect, Process, and Analyze the Data***
   *Data collection consumes a large portion of the research budget. The processing of data involves **reviewing the data for accuracy and completeness** and then **tabulating or coding the results**. Most data analysis is conducted using computers.*

5. ***Present the Results***

*At the end of the research process, you communicate your results to management through an **oral presentation** and/or a **written report**. Ensure that you keep the presentation simple—your audience is there to be informed, not won over by your technical prowess.*

2. Bradley has been asked to deliver his "Marketing" presentation to the local chapter of the AASP (Association of Advertising and Sales Professionals), and Gayle and her client have agreed. The association has rented the lecture theater on the Springs College campus for an expected attendance of 200 members. They've also asked Bradley to produce a copy of his presentation on 35 mm slides so they can send it to their head office in Atlanta. Bradley decides to change the presentation's template for use as a 35 mm slide and add a copyright notice to the bottom of the audience handouts. The notice reads, "Copyright © 1997 by Gayle Fanning and Bradley Neumann." He outputs the presentation for 35 mm slides to a print file called "Marketing-35mm" on the Advantage Diskette.

3. Wally Fong had to dodge several people and trays to make it safely to where Bradley was sitting in the cafeteria. He politely asked to join Bradley and quickly took the seat across from him at the small round table. "I understand that you're the new guy who is taking over for Gayle. I'm Wally Fong, an instructor in computer sciences. I was communicating with Gayle over the Net and she mentioned that you had done some outstanding work in PowerPoint." Bradley smiled shyly and went back to his half-eaten salad. "I'd like to get your help on developing a PowerPoint presentation that reviews some of the newest operating system software." After further clarification and two espressos, Bradley agreed to help Wally with his project.

Given that Bradley's time was limited, he encouraged Wally to develop the content for the presentation using the AutoContent Wizard. He would then take Wally's work and add clip art images, slide timings, transitions, and build slides. To get Wally started, the two men developed an outline for the presentation together, as provided below:

General	Operating System Software Review
	▬ Prepared by Wally Fong, Computer Sciences, and Bradley Neumann, Business Admin.
Introduction	This presentation reviews the strengths and weaknesses of operating system software currently available for the personal computer.
Topics of Discussion	The main ideas to be discussed include looking at three operating system software solutions: Windows, OS/2 Warp, and System 7.5.

Topic One	Windows
	• Graphical user interface (GUI)
	• 32-bit, preemptive multitasking
	• Plug and Play technology
	• Access to the Internet and the Microsoft Online Network
Topic Two	OS/2 Warp
	• Graphical user interface (GUI) based on System Object Model (SOM)
	• 32-bit, preemptive multitasking
	• Runs DOS, Windows, and OS/2 applications software in separate sessions
Topic Three	System 7.5
	• Most mature and developed of all graphical user interfaces (GUI)
	• 32-bit preemptive multitasking
	• Excellent for graphics and multimedia
	• Runs on new PowerPC platform
Real Life	The User's Perspective
	• Will it run the applications I need to use?
	• Will it provide a more stable environment?
	• What are the real costs of switching from my current operating system software?
What This Means	Learn to review the features of an operating system software with respect to your computing needs. Do not get consumed by the advertisements pervading every trade journal that promise the world for only $99. The real costs are much greater than this!
Next Steps	1. Build a checklist of the features you require in operating system software.
	2. Review each operating system based on this checklist.
	3. Consider all the costs associated with switching or upgrading your system software.

As Wally, create a presentation using the AutoContent Wizard. Next, assume the role of Bradley and apply an on-screen template and special visual effects to the presentation. Save your work as "Operating Systems" to your Data Files location.

Microsoft PowerPoint 97 Toolbar Summary

STANDARD

FORMATTING

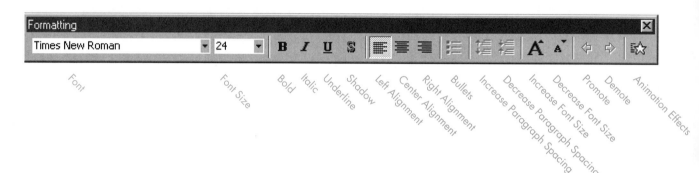

DRAWING

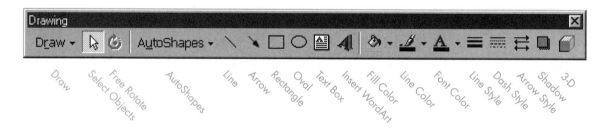

PICTURE

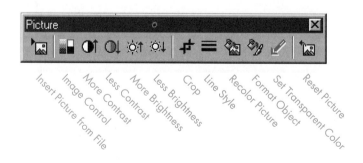

ANIMATE

OUTLINE

Index

The page numbers in boldface indicate Quick Reference procedures.